Melted
CHEESE

Melted CHEESE

GLORIOUSLY GOOEY RECIPES, FROM FONDUE TO GRILLED CHEESE & PASTA BAKE TO POTATO GRATIN

RYLAND PETERS & SMALL
LONDON • NEW YORK

Senior Designer Toni Kay
Commissioning Editor
 Alice Sambrook
Production Mai-Ling Collyer
Art Director Leslie Harrington
Editorial Director Julia Charles
Publisher Cindy Richards
Indexer Vanessa Bird

First published in 2019 by
Ryland Peters & Small
20–21 Jockey's Fields, London
WC1R 4BW
and
341 E 116th St, New York NY
10029
www.rylandpeters.com

10 9 8 7 6 5 4 3 2 1

Recipe collection compiled by
Julia Charles

ISBN: 978-1-78879-164-9

Printed in China

NOTES:
• Both British (Metric) and
American (Imperial plus US cups)
measurements are included in
these recipes for your convenience,
however it is important to work
with one set of measurements
and not alternate between the
 two within a recipe.
• All spoon measurements are
level unless otherwise specified.
• All eggs are medium (UK) or
large (US), unless specified as
large, in which case US extra-
large should be used. Uncooked
or partially cooked eggs should
not be served to the very old,
frail, young children, pregnant
women or those with compromised
immune systems.
• Ovens should be preheated
to the specified temperatures.
We recommend using an oven
thermometer. If using a fan-assisted
oven, adjust temperatures according
to the manufacturer's instructions.
• When a recipe calls for the
grated zest of citrus fruit, buy
unwaxed fruit and wash well
before using. If you can only find
treated fruit, scrub well in warm
soapy water before using.

CONTENTS

INTRODUCTION

Perfect for making a big night in an indulgent experience to remember, this book features over 70 decadent recipes just oozing with melted golden goodness. From grilled cheese sandwiches, designed for gorging on all alone, to big pots of fondue for sharing with friends, there is no shame in enjoying melted cheese for one, but equally it is good to share the love, too. In these pages, you'll discover a multitude of ways to serve your favourite comfort food, in various delicious guises.

It is no coincidence that some of the most-loved dishes from all over the world include melted cheese in one form or another. Switzerland has given us fondue and raclette, Italy offers cheese-loaded pizza and pasta and Mexican cuisine brings nachos and enchiladas to the party. UK favourites include Welsh rarebit and cauliflower cheese and who could forget the all-American cheeseburger or mac 'n' cheese? Of course, we all now mix and match these melted cheese favourites all over the world and make our own variations on these popular dishes. No matter how many evolutions they seem go through, the one common theme of copious amounts of melted cheese stays the same!

But why are we so captivated by this alluring foodstuff to the point of cultural obsession? It could be the way it goes stringy when you take a big bite, or the way it bubbles and turns golden when you remove it from the oven. Maybe it's the creamy texture coupled with the unique savoury taste, or the type of warm, comforting, carby dishes it goes on. Whatever it is, our age-old love affair with melted cheese shows no signs of slowing.

A BRIEF HISTORY OF MELTED CHEESE

It's near on impossible to pinpoint the moment in history that people discovered smothering food in melted cheese to be an excellent idea. The discovery of a very basic early form of cheese itself is thought to date back to around 8,000 BC. It probably occurred by accident, in a country with a warm climate, when milk was transported inside animal membranes. These membranes contain natural enzymes that would eventually turn the milk into cheese.

Making cheese began to be considered something of an art-form in the Roman era, and it was served to the rich. The cheeses that we are more familiar with today started to be produced in the cooler climate of Europe in the Middle Ages. The first cheese factory was constructed in 1815 in Switzerland, and once scientists discovered how to pasteurise it, mass production of cheese sky-rocketed worldwide. Processed American cheese was first invented around 1910 and this type of cheese became such a hit, partly because it melts very well indeed. The cheeseburger is said to have been invented in America in 1926 and fondue was popularized as a Swiss national dish by the Swiss Cheese Union in the 1930s as a way of increasing cheese consumption, such is the increased allure of cheese when it is melted. In more recent decades, hand-made artisan cheeses with

incredible flavour are again favoured, as people have discovered how best to cook with and flavour-match the various types available.

THE SCIENCE BEHIND MELTED CHEESE

Cheese itself is usually an emulsion of dairy fat and water, bound together by proteins. But different cheeses have different additional ingredients and different ratios of fat and water, and they therefore have differing optimum melting points. The first stage of melting occurs in most cheeses at about 32°C (90°F), when the milk fat starts to soften. The cheese may start to 'sweat' or become pliable. As heat increases, the protein bonds break down too and the whole thing completely collapses into a gooey puddle.

There are four main things that affect how easily a cheese melts, these are:
- *moisture content*
- *fat content*
- *acidity content*
- *age*

Softer cheeses with a high moisture content melt completely at around 54°C (130°F), for aged lower-moisture cheeses it's 65°C (150°F) and hard, dry cheeses need to reach up to about 82°C (180°F).

Generally speaking, the higher the moisture content, the better the melt. The increased water content allows cheeses to completely liquefy into a pool of cheese, whereas this is harder in cheeses with very little water. Cheeses loaded with fat make perfect melters (just one reason that full-fat cheese is always preferable) and cheeses with naturally occurring acid are able to dissolve more easily under heat. Finally, cheeses that are more aged sometimes have a tougher time melting as the proteins become more tightly bound as time goes on.

TIPS AND TRICKS FOR MELTING CHEESE LIKE A PRO

Granted, some cheeses melt more easily than others but, as a cook, there are still definitely things you can do to make sure your melted cheese is the best it can possibly be:

Pick the right cheese for the right recipe
Different cheeses respond to heat in different ways. Some become liquid, some become stringy and some just soften or don't really melt at all. It's fine to mix and match the cheeses in these recipes, just make sure you refer to the guide on page 13 to help you pick something that it right for your recipe.

Choose your cooking method wisely

The oven is a great way to melt cheese because it provides a nice even heat and you can easily control the temperature. Alternatively, the grill/ broiler is perfect for turning cheesy toppings golden. It is not usually a good idea to melt cheese in the microwave, as this produces an uneven heat, which will leave some bits of cheese scalding hot and others lukewarm and not fully melted.

Treat it gently

Melting cheese requires a delicate touch. Don't stir too roughly when making cheese sauces and don't heat your cheese too quickly at a fierce temperature. Heating cheese too fiercely can sometimes result in its proteins separating from the water and fat rather than nicely emulsifying, leaving you with rubbery cheese and pools of oil. This is at worst a bit disappointing on a pizza, but it's a full-blown disaster in a cheese sauce or a fondue.

Bring it to room temperature first

If it's fridge-cold all the way through, your cheese will take longer to break down. Bringing it to room temperature before cooking gives it a head start and lessens the dramatic rapid change in temperature, which could result in the liquid and fat separation.

Grating/shredding is good

Grating or shredding cheese that is going to be melted is a wise move, as it gives more surface area for the heat to permeate and thus the melting process will be quicker. It also means you will have perfectly even pieces which will all melt at the same rate. A cheese plane slicer is also a great tool for making thin, evenly sized slices ready for melting.

Acidity and starch are your friends

Adding certain other ingredients can improve the texture of your melted cheese. White wine or lemon juice are both high in acidity and can be added to fondues, sauces or soups to help keep the texture silky smooth. Starches such as flour or cornflour/cornstarch also act as a barrier against clumps.

Keep it hot

If you let melted cheese cool too much before serving, it will lose its beautiful oozing texture and become firm and congealed. Serve immediately for best results.

Use processed cheese for a fail-safe option

Processed cheese is a quick and easy

melter – it has a low melting point and, no matter how much you overheat it, will stay smooth and flowing. It might not have the best flavour, but it's great on things like barbecued/grilled burgers where you can't control the fierce heat as easily.

WHICH CHEESES MELT BEST?

Mozzarella With a very high moisture content, mozzarella melts quickly and easily. It is famous for its amazing 'pull' – the long stringy, stretchy bits. With a mild, creamy taste it is a great 'topper' though doesn't work as well in soups or sauces. Try it on pizza, pasta, with meatballs or in grilled cheese sandwiches.

Cheddar A go-to option for lovers of melted cheese, this great all-rounder works in pretty much everything. Available from young and mild to aged and sharp in flavour, the sharper and more aged the cheese, the more heat it will need to melt. Try it in soups, béchamel sauces, toasties, burgers or really anything you like!

Gruyère High in acid, this cheese is favoured for its gloriously smooth melt as well as its unique and moreish salty-sweet-nutty taste. Known as one of the alpine cheeses (along with emmental and comté), this is perfect in fondue, for topping French onion soup or for adding to gratins.

Camembert This cheese is a king amongst melters. It goes exceptionally creamy and most people prefer to serve it straight-up out of the box, with crudités or crusty bread for dipping.

Brie With a very high moisture and fat content, this is another excellent melter. Try it in sandwiches or burgers. It goes exceptionally well with bacon and piquant condiments.

Fontina This buttery and mildy tangy Italian cheese turns into a beautifully oozy mess when melted. It goes well on all manner on things, from inside sandwiches to topping potatoes, just remember to remove the rind first.

Raclette Another superstar of the melted cheese world, the word raclette is the name of an incredible Swiss cheese and the dish you use it for. If you want to serve raclette at home, you will need to invest in a raclette grill – see page 135 for more details and the recipe.

BREAD

Grilled Cheese • Toasties • Panini • Pizza

THREE CHEESE TOASTIE

WHAT ELEVATES THIS BASIC TOASTIE ABOVE THE CROWD IS THE RIGHT BLEND OF CHEESE: MELTY MOZZARELLA, SOMETHING INTENSE LIKE A GOOD MATURE/SHARP CHEDDAR AND EMMENTAL/SWISS CHEESE FOR A HINT OF NUTTINESS. YUM!

4 large slices white bread
unsalted butter, softened
70 g/scant 1 cup grated/shredded
    Lincolnshire Poacher or mature/sharp Cheddar
70 g/scant 1 cup grated/shredded Emmental/Swiss cheese
125 g/4½ oz. mozzarella, sliced

Serves 2

Butter each of the bread slices on one side.

Without turning the heat on, place two slices of the bread in a large, non-stick frying pan/skillet, butter-side down. If you can only accommodate one slice in your pan, you'll need to cook one sandwich at a time. Sprinkle the slices in the pan with half of the Lincolnshire Poacher or Cheddar in an even layer. Top with half of the mozzarella slices, then sprinkle half of the Emmental/Swiss cheese on top. Top with the remaining bread slices, butter-side up.

Turn the heat to medium and cook the first side for 3–5 minutes until it turns a deep golden colour. Carefully turn with a spatula and cook on the second side for 2–3 minutes, or until deep golden brown all over.

Remove from the frying pan/skillet, transfer to a plate and cut the sandwiches into quarters. Let cool for a few minutes before serving. Serve with a nice hot bowl of tomato soup, if liked.

BASIC GRILLED CHEESE

THIS IS THE BASIC GRILLED CHEESE METHOD, WHICH CAN BE USED AS A BLUEPRINT FOR ALL SORTS OF EXPERIMENTATION. IT'S A GOOD IDEA TO START WITH TWO RELATIVELY MILD CHEESES, SUCH AS A MILD CHEDDAR AND MONTEREY JACK.

4 large slices white bread
unsalted butter, softened
300 g/3¼ cups mixed grated/shredded mild cheeses,
    such as mild Cheddar, Gruyére, Monterey Jack or Gouda

Serves 2

Butter each of the bread slices on one side.

Without turning the heat on, place two slices of the bread in a large, non-stick frying pan/skillet, butter-side down. If you can only accommodate one slice in your pan, you'll need to cook one sandwich at a time. Top each slice with half of the grated/shredded cheese, but be careful not to let too much cheese fall into the pan. Top with the final pieces of bread, butter-side up.

Turn the heat to medium and cook for about 3–4 minutes on the first side, then carefully turn with a large spatula and cook on the second side for 2–3 minutes until the sandwiches are golden brown all over and all the cheese is visibly melted.

Remove from the frying pan/skillet and cut the sandwiches in half. Let cool for a few minutes before serving. Dunk to your heart's content in a lovely steaming bowl of tomato soup.

RED ONION CHUTNEY & CHEDDAR TOASTIE

CHEDDAR AND CHUTNEY IS A WINNING COMBINATION, BUT FOR BEST RESULTS, BE SURE TO USE A REALLY GUTSY MATURE/SHARP CHEDDAR HERE. THE CHUTNEY NEEDS TO HAVE A GOOD BALANCE OF SWEETNESS AND TARTNESS TO MAKE THIS WORK PERFECTLY, SO BE SURE TO TASTE AND ADJUST BEFORE ASSEMBLING THE SANDWICHES.

4 slices white bread
unsalted butter, softened
150 g/1¾ cups grated/shredded
  mature/sharp Cheddar

FOR THE QUICK CHUTNEY
2 red onions, halved and
  thinly sliced
2 tablespoons vegetable oil
good pinch of salt
1 tablespoon light brown sugar
2 tablespoons wine vinegar
2 tablespoons balsamic vinegar

Serves 2

For the chutney, in a small non-stick frying pan/skillet, combine the onions and oil over a medium-high heat and cook, stirring occasionally, until caramelized. Add the remaining chutney ingredients, reduce the heat to a simmer and cook until the mixture is sticky but still somewhat liquid. Taste and adjust the seasoning, adding more sugar for sweetness or vinegar for tartness, as required.

Butter each of the bread slices on one side and set aside.

Without turning the heat on, place two slices of bread in a large, ridged griddle/stove-top pan, butter-side down. If you can only fit one slice in your pan, you'll need to cook one sandwich at a time. Spread generously with some of the chutney and sprinkle each slice with half the grated/shredded cheese in an even layer. Cover each slice with another bread slice, butter-side up.

Turn the heat to medium and cook the first side for 3–4 minutes until it turns a deep golden colour, pressing gently with a spatula. Carefully turn with the spatula and cook on the second side for 2–3 minutes, or until deep golden brown all over. To achieve the lovely criss-cross pattern, turn the sandwiches over again, rotate them 90° to the left or right and cook for a final 2–3 minutes.

Remove from the pan, transfer to a plate and cut the sandwiches in half. Let cool for a few minutes before serving with extra chutney.

NOTE Leftover chutney, if any, can be kept in the refrigerator in a sealed container.

LEEK & GRUYÈRE GRILLED CHEESE

A STRONG FRENCH GRUYÈRE MELTS SO BEAUTIFULLY AND IS CERTAINLY UP THERE AMONG THE FINEST OF CHEESES. IF A GRILLED CHEESE SANDWICH COULD BE FRENCH, IT WOULD BE THIS ONE – SIMPLE YET ELEGANT. SERVE WITH A GLASS OF CHILLED WHITE WINE FROM THE LOIRE VALLEY.

4 slices white bread
unsalted butter, softened
wholegrain Dijon mustard
250 g/2 cups grated/
    shredded Gruyère

FOR THE LEEKS
1 large leek, rinsed and sliced
    thinly into rounds
1 teaspoon vegetable oil
1 tablespoon unsalted butter
½ teaspoon dried thyme
6 tablespoons dry white wine
salt and freshly ground
    black pepper

Serves 2

For the leeks, in a non-stick frying pan/skillet, combine the leek, oil, butter and thyme over a medium-high heat and cook, stirring occasionally, until soft and golden. Season well, add the wine and simmer until the liquid evaporates. Taste and adjust the seasoning. Set aside.

Butter each of the bread slices on one side, then spread two of the slices with mustard on the non-buttered side.

Without turning the heat on, place two slices of the bread in a large, ridged griddle/stove-top pan, butter-side down. If you can only fit one slice in your pan, you'll need to cook one sandwich at a time. Spoon half of the leek mixture over each slice and sprinkle over half the grated/shredded cheese in an even layer. Cover with another bread slice each, mustard-side down.

Turn the heat to medium and cook the first side for 3–5 minutes until it turns a deep golden colour, pressing gently with a spatula. Carefully turn with the spatula and cook on the second side for 2–3 minutes, or until deep golden brown all over.

Remove from the ridged griddle/stovetop pan, transfer to a plate and cut the sandwiches in half. Let cool for a few minutes before serving.

VARIATION Other good French cheeses to try here include Beaufort, Comté and Raclette.

MUSHROOM & FONTINA TOASTIE

HERE, TANGY BALSAMIC MUSHROOMS OFFER AN EARTHY ACCOMPANIMENT TO THE RICH
MELTED FONTINA. LIKE MOST GRILLED CHEESE SANDWICHES, THIS ONE GOES WELL WITH
TOMATO SOUP, BUT ALSO WORKS NICELY WITH A HEARTY CREAM OF MUSHROOM SOUP.

4 slices granary/granary-style
   bread
unsalted butter, softened
150g/1¼ cups grated/shredded
   Fontina, or use thin slices

FOR THE MUSHROOMS
2 tablespoons unsalted butter
1 tablespoon vegetable oil
125 g/1⅔ cups white mushrooms,
   thinly sliced
1 shallot, diced
½ teaspoon dried thyme
3 tablespoons balsamic vinegar
1 teaspoon red wine vinegar
salt and freshly ground
   black pepper

Serves 2

For the mushrooms, in a non-stick frying pan/skillet, combine
the butter, oil, mushrooms, shallot and thyme over a medium-high
heat and cook, stirring occasionally, until everything is soft and deep
golden in colour. Season well, add the vinegars and simmer until
the liquid almost evaporates. Taste and adjust the seasoning.

Butter each of the bread slices on one side.

Without turning the heat on, place two slices of the bread in a large,
non-stick frying pan/skillet, butter-side down. If you can only fit one
slice in your pan/skillet, you'll need to cook one sandwich at a time.
Spoon over half of the mushrooms and sprinkle half of the grated/
shredded cheese on top in an even layer. Cover each slice with
another bread slice, butter-side up.

Turn the heat to medium and cook the first side for
3–5 minutes until it turns a deep golden colour, pressing
gently with a spatula. Carefully turn with the spatula
and cook on the second side for 2–3 minutes,
or until deep golden brown all over.

Remove from the frying pan/skillet,
transfer to a plate and
cut the sandwiches
in half. Let cool
for a few minutes
before serving.

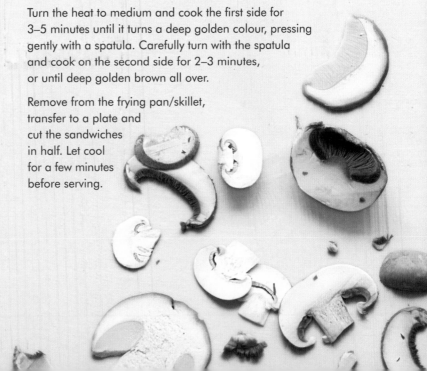

PUTTANESCA & MOZZARELLA FOCACCIA

large round or square focaccia, halved lengthways and widthways
extra-virgin olive oil
4 tablespoons black olive paste
2 tablespoons sun-dried tomato paste
4–6 tablespoons passata/strained tomatoes
2 fresh mozzarella balls, drained and thinly sliced
2 teaspoons dried oregano
2 tablespoons grated/shredded Parmesan
2–3 tablespoons capers, drained
good pinch of chilli/hot red pepper flakes
few fresh basil leaves, torn

Serves 2-4

HALFWAY BETWEEN A PIZZA AND A PASTA SAUCE, THIS SANDWICH BRINGS TOGETHER CLASSIC ITALIAN INGREDIENTS. FRESH MOZZARELLA MELTS BEST, SO BE SURE TO USE THIS IF YOU CAN AND YOU'LL BE IN FOR A REAL TREAT.

Brush the outsides of the focaccia halves with olive oil and arrange oil-side down on a clean work surface or chopping board.

Spread two of the non-oiled sides generously with the olive paste. Spread the other two non-oiled sides with the sun-dried tomato paste, then top with the passata/strained tomatoes. Divide the mozzarella slices between the tomato-coated sides. Sprinkle over the oregano, Parmesan, capers and chilli/hot red pepper flakes. Scatter over a few basil leaves. Top with the olive oil-coated bread, oiled side up.

Without turning the heat on, place the two sandwiches in a large, non-stick frying pan/skillet. If you can only fit one sandwich in your pan/skillet, you'll need to cook one sandwich at a time.

Turn the heat to medium and cook the first side for 4–5 minutes, then carefully turn with a large spatula and cook the other side for 2–3 minutes, pressing down gently with the spatula until golden brown all over.

Remove from the frying pan/skillet, transfer to a wooden chopping board or a plate and cut the sandwiches in half. Let cool for a few minutes before serving.

KIMCHI & MONTEREY JACK TOASTIE

MELTED CHEESE IS COMPLEMENTED BY SOUR OR TANGY INGREDIENTS THAT CUT THROUGH THE RICHNESS. HERE, KIMCHI, A SPICED KOREAN CONDIMENT OF FERMENTED PICKLED CABBAGE, DOES JUST THAT TO PERFECTION. THE COMBINATION MAY SOUND STRANGE AT FIRST, BUT IT'S FANTASTIC. THERE'S A GOOD REASON WHY KIMCHI IS TAKING OFF AROUND THE WORLD!

4 slices white bread,
   crusts removed
unsalted butter, softened
60 g/½ cup kimchi
150 g/1¾ cups grated/shredded
   mild cheese, such as Monterey
   Jack or mild Cheddar

Serves 2

Butter each of the bread slices on one side and set aside.

Pat the kimchi dry with paper towels to remove excess moisture and chop.

Without turning the heat on, put two slices of the bread in a large, heavy-based non-stick frying pan/skillet, butter-side down. If you can only fit one slice in your pan/skillet, you'll need to cook one sandwich at a time. Top with half the kimchi and sprinkle over half the grated/shredded cheese in an even layer. Cover each with another bread slice, butter-side up.

Turn the heat to medium and cook the first side for 3–5 minutes until it turns a deep golden colour, pressing gently with a spatula. Carefully turn with the spatula and cook on the second side for 2–3 minutes, or until deep golden brown all over.

Remove from the frying pan/skillet, transfer to a plate and cut in half. Let cool for a few minutes before serving. Repeat for the remaining sandwich if necessary.

NOTE Vegetarians should note that kimchi often contains fish as part of the seasoning.

BRIE & APPLE-CRANBERRY TOASTIE

THIN SLICES OF BRIE MELT MORE SUCCESSFULLY SO A GOOD TIP WITH THIS RECIPE IS TO SLICE THE CHEESE WHEN IT IS CHILLED (WHICH IS EASIER), THEN BRING THE SLICES TO ROOM TEMPERATURE BEFORE USING IN THE SANDWICH. ALSO, REMOVE THE RIND BECAUSE IT DOES NOT MELT WELL. FEEL FREE TO SUBSTITUTE WHOLE-WHEAT BREAD IF WALNUT BREAD IS NOT AVAILABLE.

4–8 slices walnut bread, depending on size of loaf
unsalted butter, softened
about 180g/6 oz. ripe chilled Brie, rind removed, sliced thinly or finely diced

FOR THE APPLE-CRANBERRY SAUCE

300 g/3 cups cranberries, fresh or frozen
juice of 1 orange
1 small tart cooking apple, such as Cox, peeled and diced
about 3 tablespoons caster/ granulated sugar or more to taste

Serves 2

For the apple-cranberry sauce, combine all the ingredients in a saucepan over a low heat. Stir the mixture often, until the sugar dissolves and the cranberries begin to pop and disintegrate. If the mixture is too dry, add a small amount of water. Cover and simmer gently until the cranberries are tender and the mixture has a jam-like consistency; keep checking to see if the mixture is too dry – if it is, add water bit-by-bit to prevent the mixture from thickening and burning. Taste and adjust the sweetness to your liking. Set aside until needed.

Butter the bread slices on one side.

Without turning the heat on, place two slices of the bread in a large, heavy-based, non-stick frying pan/skillet, butter-side down. If you can't fit two slices side-by-side in the pan/skillet, you'll need to cook them in two batches. Spread the slices generously with some of the apple-cranberry sauce, then top with Brie slices. Cover with the remaining bread slices, butter-side up.

Turn the heat to medium and cook the first side for 3–5 minutes until it turns a deep golden colour, pressing gently with a spatula. Carefully turn with the spatula and cook on the second side for 2–3 minutes, or until deep golden brown all over.

Remove from the frying pan/skillet, transfer to a plate and cut in half. Let cool for a few minutes before serving along with extra apple-cranberry sauce.

NOTE Leftover apple-cranberry sauce can be kept in the refrigerator in a sealed container.

WELSH RAREBIT

AN EXQUISITE VEHICLE FOR SOME WONDERFUL, TYPICAL BRITISH INGREDIENTS: INTENSE
CHEDDAR, TANGY WORCESTERSHIRE SAUCE AND MELLOW MUSTARD POWDER, ALL BOUND
TOGETHER WITH THE BITTERNESS OF ALE. INCREDIBLY SIMPLE AND DEEPLY SATISFYING,
YOU CAN SERVE THIS ANYTIME OF DAY OR NIGHT.

4 slices ciabatta or sourdough
   bread
30 g/2 tablespoons unsalted
   butter, plus extra for spreading
30 g/3 tablespoons plain/
   all-purpose flour
125 ml/½ cup ale, at room
   temperature
1 teaspoon mustard powder
150 g/1¾ cups grated/shredded
   mature/sharp Cheddar
1 tablespoon Worcestershire sauce
pinch of ground cayenne pepper

Serves 2

Butter each of the bread slices on one side and arrange them
buttered-side down on a clean work surface or chopping board.

In a small saucepan over a low heat, combine the butter and
flour, stirring until melted. Pour the ale in gradually and stir
continuously until the mixture thickens. Add the mustard powder,
cheese, Worcestershire sauce and cayenne pepper and stir to
just melt the cheese before taking the pan off the heat.

Put two slices of the bread in a large frying pan/skillet, butter-
side down. If you can't fit two pieces of bread in the pan/skillet,
cook them one at a time. Top each slice with half of the cheese,
then enclose with the other slices of bread, butter-side up.

Turn the heat to medium and cook for 3–4 minutes on the first
side, then carefully turn with a large spatula and cook on the
other side for 1–2 minutes more until golden brown all over.

Remove from the pan/skillet and cut in half. Let cool for a few
minutes before serving.

MEATBALL, GARLIC TOMATO SAUCE & FONTINA CIABATTA

FONTINA IS A CHAMPION IN THE WORLD OF MELTED CHEESE, HERE IT OOZES AROUND THE SPHERES OF SEASONED BEEF TO PERFECTION.

1 large ciabatta, cut into 3 thick slices then cut widthways
4–6 slices or about 250 g/2¼ cups grated/shredded Fontina

FOR THE MEATBALLS
225 g/8 oz. minced/ground meat, half beef and half Italian sausage
30 g/½ cup fresh breadcrumbs
1 teaspoon dried oregano
1 teaspoon dried rosemary
pinch of chilli/hot red pepper flakes, or more to taste
1 egg, beaten
2 tablespoons milk, or more if necessary
1 teaspoon salt
freshly ground black pepper

FOR THE GARLIC TOMATO SAUCE
3 garlic cloves, crushed but not peeled
extra-virgin olive oil
200 g/7 oz. passata/ strained tomatoes
1 tablespoon unsalted butter
pinch of caster/granulated sugar
salt and ground black pepper

baking sheet lined with parchment paper

Serves 3

Preheat the oven to 190°C (375°F) Gas 5.

In a mixing bowl, combine all the meatball ingredients and mix well. The mixture should be firm enough to form into balls and moist enough so they are not dry; add more milk as required. Form them into 8–10 golf ball-sized balls and arrange on the baking sheet. Bake until browned and cooked though, 20–30 minutes. Remove from the oven and let cool slightly. Slice in half and set aside until needed.

Meanwhile, prepare the sauce. Coat the garlic cloves lightly with oil, place in a small ovenproof dish such as a ramekin, and roast, at the same time as the meatballs, for 10–15 minutes, until golden and tender. Be careful not to let the garlic burn. Remove the garlic from the oven, slip the cloves from their skins and chop finely. In a small saucepan, melt the butter. Add the passata/strained tomatoes, garlic, sugar and salt and pepper. Simmer for 15 minutes. Taste and adjust the seasoning. Keep warm until needed.

Coat the outsides of the bread slices with oil. It's best to assemble the sandwiches just before cooking, in a large, heavy-based, non-stick frying pan/skillet. Depending on the size of your pan/skillet, you may need to cook them in batches. If space allows, put the three slices of bread, oil-side down, in the pan/skillet. Arrange half the cheese slices on top of them, then top with the meatball halves, dividing the pieces evenly among the three sandwiches. Coat the inside of the remaining bread pieces generously with the tomato sauce and place on top of the sandwiches to enclose, oil-side up.

Turn the heat to medium and cook the first side for 3–4 minutes until deep golden, pressing gently with a spatula. Very carefully turn with a large spatula and cook on the other side, for 2–3 minutes more or until deep golden brown all over. Remove from the pan/skillet and let cool for a few minutes before serving. If the sandwich isn't holding together well, insert a small wooden skewer through the middle.

PHILLY CHEESESTEAK SANDWICH

THE AUTHENTIC VERSION OF THIS SANDWICH CALLS FOR MELTED CHEESE TO TOP THE MEAT AND ONIONS, SO GRILLING IT IS A DEPARTURE FROM TRADITION. THE CHEESE CAN EITHER BE SWISS CHEESE OR PROCESSED CHEESE, BUT THIS RECIPE USES BOTH. THE DILL PICKLE IS NOT PART OF THE REAL THING, BUT IT ADDS A WELCOME TANG AND CRUNCH TO THIS SUBSTANTIAL CLASSIC.

1 ciabatta or 2 long white rolls
3 tablespoons spreadable
  processed cheese, such as
  Dairylea or Kraft
vegetable oil
6–8 slices Emmental/Swiss cheese
2 large gherkins/pickles, thinly
  sliced lengthwise, plus extra
  to serve

FOR THE ONIONS
2 large onions, thinly sliced
1 tablespoon unsalted butter
2 tablespoons vegetable oil
salt and freshly ground
  black pepper

FOR THE BEEF
1 tablespoon vegetable oil
350 g/12½ oz. minute/cube
  steak, thinly sliced
salt and freshly ground
  black pepper

Serves 2

For the onions, in a frying pan/skillet, combine the onions with the butter and vegetable oil. Cook over a medium heat, stirring occasionally, until deep golden brown, about 10 minutes. Season lightly and transfer to a small bowl.

For the beef, in the same pan/skillet, add another 1 tablespoon oil and heat. When hot but not smoking, add the beef and cook for 2–3 minutes, stirring often until cooked through. Season lightly and set aside.

To assemble, cut the ciabatta in half at the middle to obtain two even pieces, and slice these in half widthways. Take the bottom halves and spread the insides with processed cheese. With a small brush, coat the outsides of the bread, tops and bottoms, lightly with oil.

Assemble just before cooking, in a large, heavy-based, non-stick frying pan/skillet. Depending on the size of your pan/skillet, you may need to cook one sandwich at a time.

Put the plain slices of bread, oil-side down, in the pan/skillet. Arrange half the Emmental/Swiss cheese slices on top of these bread slices, then top each bread slice with half the beef and half the onions. Cover with the processed cheese-coated bread slice and place on top of the sandwich to enclose, oil-side up.

Turn the heat to medium and cook the first side for 3–5 minutes until deep golden, pressing gently with a large spatula. Carefully turn with the spatula and cook on the other side, for 2–3 minutes more or until deep golden brown all over.

Remove from the pan and cut in half. Let cool for a few minutes before serving. Repeat for the remaining sandwich if necessary.

CHILLI BACON GRILLED CHEESE

THIS RECIPE INCLUDES A VERY QUICK, CHEAT'S CHILLI CON CARNE, WHICH IS PRETTY PERFECT, BUT IF YOU HAVE SOME LEFTOVER CHILLI CON CARNE, THIS SANDWICH WILL PUT IT TO GOOD USE. FOR THE CHEESE, ANY NUTTY-TASTING ALPINE CHEESE WORKS WELL HERE, OR EVEN A DUTCH CHEESE, BUT NOTHING TOO STRONG AS IT WILL BE OVERPOWERED BY THE SPICY MEAT.

6 rashers/slices streaky/
   American bacon
4 slices bread
unsalted butter, softened
2–4 slices or 150 g/2 cups grated/
   shredded Emmental/
   Swiss cheese

**FOR THE QUICK
CHILLI CON CARNE**
1 small onion, finely chopped
1 tablespoon vegetable oil
150 g/5½ oz. minced/
   ground beef
1 teaspoon dried oregano
1 tablespoon ground cumin
½ teaspoon chilli/hot red pepper
   flakes, or more to taste
½ teaspoon ground cayenne
   pepper, or more to taste
200 g/7 oz. passata/
   strained tomatoes
400-g/14-oz. can black beans,
   drained
salt and freshly ground
   black pepper

Serves 2

For the chilli con carne, combine the onion and oil in a frying pan/skillet over a medium heat and cook until soft and golden. Add the beef, oregano, spices, salt and pepper, and cook, stirring occasionally, until browned. Add the passata/strained tomatoes and beans, and simmer gently for at least 15 minutes. The mixture should be thick but not too thick; add a splash of water if necessary. Taste and adjust the seasoning.

Meanwhile, fry the bacon until crispy. Pat dry on paper towels and set aside.

Spread softened butter on the bread slices on one side.

This is easiest if assembled in a large heavy-based non-stick frying pan/skillet. Depending on the size of your pan, you may need to cook one sandwich at a time. If space allows, put two slices of bread in the pan/skillet, butter-side down. Top each slice with half of the cheese, half of the bacon and half of the chilli con carne. It is best to drop the chilli con carne in spoonfuls and then spread the blobs out to the edges, gently, without disturbing the cheese beneath too much. Enclose with the two remaining bread slices, butter-side up.

Turn the heat to medium and cook the first side for 3–5 minutes until deep golden, pressing gently with a spatula. Carefully turn with a large spatula and cook on the other side for 2–3 minutes more or until deep golden brown all over.

Remove from the pan, transfer to a plate and cut in half. Let cool for a few minutes before serving. Repeat for the remaining sandwich if necessary.

BURGER SCAMORZA

SCAMORZA IS AN ITALIAN SMOKED CHEESE, SIMILAR TO MOZZARELLA IN THAT IT HAS THE SAME BEAUTIFUL MELTING QUALITY, BUT WITH A LITTLE MORE PUNCH. THE BURGER FOR THIS SANDWICH NEEDS TO BE THIN-ISH FOR EASE OF COOKING AND EATING, SO IT IS FEASIBLE TO ALLOW TWO PER PERSON IF APPETITES ARE HEARTY. SERVE WITH FRIES, NATURALLY.

2 white burger buns
vegetable oil
300 g/10½ oz. scamorza
    or mozzarella, sliced
tomato ketchup, for serving
gherkin/pickle spears, for serving

FOR THE BURGERS
250 g/9 oz. minced/ground beef
1 small onion, grated/shredded
½ teaspoon garlic powder
dash of Worcestershire sauce,
    optional
½ teaspoon salt
freshly ground black pepper

Serves 2

Slice the burger buns in half widthways. Brush the bun halves lightly on the outside with vegetable oil. Set aside.

For the burgers, in a mixing bowl, combine the minced/ground beef, onion, garlic powder, Worcestershire sauce (if using), salt and pepper, and mix well. Shape into two thin patties.

Heat up some vegetable oil in a large, heavy-based non-stick frying pan/skillet over a medium heat. When the pan/skillet is hot, cook the burgers for 3–5 minutes on each side, depending on how well-done you like your meat. Transfer the cooked burgers to a plate and set aside.

Clean the frying pan/skillet. If space allows, place two slices of bread, oil-side down, in the pan/skillet (without turning the heat on), but you may have to cook them one at a time if they won't fit in the pan/skillet. Top each slice with one-quarter of the scamorza or mozzarella slices, then carefully place the burger on top. Follow this with another quarter of the cheese, so that the meat is nicely surrounded by cheese. Finally, cover with another bread slice, oil-side up.

Turn the heat to medium and cook the first side for 3–5 minutes until deep golden, pressing gently with a spatula. Carefully turn with a large spatula and cook on the other side, for 2–3 minutes more or until deep golden brown all over.

Let cool for a few minutes before serving. Repeat for the remaining sandwich if necessary.

VARIATION Add two crispy, cooked streaky/American bacon rashers/slices per sandwich.

CROÛTE AU FROMAGE

HERE IS A SWISS TAKE ON CHEESE ON TOAST — AND WHAT A TAKE IT IS. NOT AN EVERYDAY
CHEESE TOASTIE, BUT A SPECIAL-OCCASION, TREAT-YOURSELF CHEESE TOASTIE. THICK-CUT BREAD
IS TOASTED IN BUTTER IN A PAN, THEN SPRINKLED WITH WHITE WINE AND COVERED IN CHEESE
(USUALLY THE RINDY ENDS OF RACLETTE OR OTHER MELTING CHEESE) AND BAKED. HEAVEN.

2 thick-cut slices of slightly stale
   white bread
2 tablespoons softened
   unsalted butter
4 tablespoons dry white wine
2 slices air-dried ham
200 g/7 oz. raclette cheese,
   especially the rindy bits, or any
   cheese you have in the fridge
gherkins and pickled silverskin
   onions, to serve

Serves 2

Heat the grill/broiler to high and heat a frying pan/skillet over
a medium heat.

Butter the bread on both sides, then fry until golden. Put each
one in a little gratin dish and sprinkle with the white wine. Top
with the slices of ham and the cheese. Pop the dishes under the
grill/broiler until golden and bubbling.

Serve the croûte with plenty of pickles on the side.

IRRESISTIBLE ITALIAN FOUR-CHEESE PIZZA

TRY MAKING THE CLASSIC "QUATTRO FORMAGGI" WITH TOP-QUALITY ITALIAN CHEESES. THE HOMEMADE VERSION IS FAR SUPERIOR THAN VERSIONS OF THIS THAT COME READY-MADE.

1⅔ cups homemade (see Note) or good-quality storebought passata/strained tomatoes
140 g/5 oz. Pecorino Toscano (rind removed), sliced
140 g/5 oz. Taleggio (rind removed) or buffalo Mozzarella, sliced
85 g/3 oz. Gorgonzola piccante, crumbled
25 g/⅓ cup freshly grated/shredded mature Parmesan
small handful of fresh oregano or basil leaves
freshly ground black pepper

FOR THE DOUGH
175 g/1¼ cups strong white bread flour
130 g/1 cup cake flour
1 teaspoon fine sea salt
1 envelope fast-action dried yeast
½ teaspoon sugar
2 tablespoons olive oil, plus extra to drizzle
about 175 ml/¾ cup hand-hot water
semolina or polenta/cornmeal, to dust the baking sheets

2 large baking sheets, lightly oiled

Makes 2 pizzas

To make the pizza dough, sift the 2 flours into a bowl along with the salt, yeast and sugar. Mix together, then form a hollow in the centre. Add the olive oil and half the hand-hot water, and stir to incorporate the flour. Gradually add as much of the remaining water as you need to pull the dough together. (It should take most of it – you need a wettish dough.) Turn the dough out onto a board and knead for 10 minutes until smooth and elastic, adding a little extra flour to prevent the dough sticking if necessary. Put the dough into a lightly oiled bowl, cover with plastic wrap, and leave in a warm place until doubled in size, about 1–1¼ hours.

Preheat the oven to 250°C (475°F) Gas 9 and sprinkle the prepared baking sheets with semolina.

Tip the dough out of the bowl and press down on it to knock out the air. Divide it in half. Pull and shape one piece of dough into a large circle, then place it on a prepared baking sheet and push it out towards the edges. (It doesn't have to be a perfect circle!) Spread half the passata/strained tomatoes over the top, then arrange half the cheeses over the top. Season with pepper. Repeat with the other piece of dough and the remaining cheese. Drizzle a little olive oil over the top of each pizza and bake in the preheated oven for 8–10 minutes until the dough has puffed up and the cheese is brown and bubbling. Garnish with oregano leaves and drizzle over a little more oil.

NOTE To make passata/strained tomatoes, heat 2 tablespoons olive oil in a large frying pan/skillet or wok, add 1 crushed garlic clove, fry for a few seconds, then add 1 level tablespoon tomato pureé/paste. Tip in 450 g/1 lb. chopped, skinned fresh ripe tomatoes and stir well. Cover with a lid and leave for 5 minutes to soften the tomatoes, then break them down with a fork or wooden spoon. Simmer, uncovered, for a further 5 minutes until the mixture is thick and pulpy. Season with salt, pepper and a pinch of sugar and let cool.

DEEP-DISH MEATBALL PIZZA PIE

CHICAGO-STYLE DEEP-DISH PIZZA IS DIFFERENT FROM ITS ITALIAN COUSIN THANKS TO ITS TALL SIDES THAT CONTAIN A RICH, OOZY CHEESE AND TOMATO FILLING. THIS PIZZA PIE IS ALSO LOADED WITH MEATBALLS FOR EVEN MORE DELICIOUSNESS.

450 g/1 lb. beef meatballs
300 g/10½ oz. fresh mozzarella, patted dry
3 tablespoons grated/shredded Parmesan

FOR THE DOUGH
¼ tablespoon fast-action dried yeast
¼ tablespoon sugar
60 g/¼ cup clarified butter or shortening
260 g/2 cups plain/ all-purpose flour
salt

FOR THE SAUCE
1 onion, finely chopped
2 tablespoons olive oil
2 garlic cloves, thinly sliced
1 x 400-g/14-oz. can tomatoes
1 pear, peeled, cored and chopped into small pieces
1 big teaspoon dried oregano
1 bay leaf

non-stick 20-cm/8-inch loose-bottomed cake pan

Serves 4

For the dough, mix 175 ml/¾ cup water with the yeast and sugar, and leave for 5 minutes. Put the yeast mixture, butter or shortening, 130 g/1 cup flour and a pinch of salt in an electric mixer with a dough hook and mix for 5 minutes. Add 100 g/¾ cup more flour and mix until a dough forms. Add the remaining flour if needed. The dough should be wet, but shouldn't stick to your hands. Put the dough in a covered bowl in the fridge to rise overnight. Remove 2–3 hours before use.

To make the sauce, lightly sauté the onion in a heavy-based casserole dish with the olive oil and garlic. When the onion is translucent and soft, add the tomatoes, pear pieces, oregano and bay leaf. Cook slowly for 1 hour, stirring occasionally, until the pear has dissolved into the tomato. Remove the bay leaf and blitz the sauce with a stick blender until smooth.

Preheat the oven to its highest setting. Brown the meatballs in a frying pan/skillet and add them to the tomato sauce. Pat out the dough in the cake pan, and up the sides. Make sure you pat the dough firmly all around the edge using your knuckles. Place three-quarters of the mozzarella in the bottom of the pan. Cover with the meatballs and tomato sauce. Top with the remaining mozzarella and the Parmesan. Bake in the preheated oven for 25–30 minutes until the crust is puffed and golden. If the inside is still at all soupy, return to the oven for another 5–10 minutes.

To serve, remove the sides of the cake pan and cut into quarters with a large knife or cake server.

PASTA

Mac 'n' Cheese • Lasagne • Oven Bakes

CLASSIC MAC 'N' CHEESE

THIS SIMPLE RECIPE MAKES A CREAMY MACARONI AND CHEESE THAT CAN BE USED AS A BASE FOR FURTHER EXPERIMENTATION. COMBINING TWO MILD CHEESES, SUCH AS CHEDDAR AND MONTEREY JACK, GIVES THIS DISH A DELICIOUS YET DELICATE DEPTH OF FLAVOUR.

handful of coarse sea salt
500 g/1 lb. 2oz. macaroni
50 g/1 cup fresh breadcrumbs
salt and freshly ground
   black pepper

FOR THE BÉCHAMEL SAUCE
50 g/3½ tablespoons unsalted
   butter
60 g/6 tablespoons plain/
   all-purpose flour
625 ml/2½ cups milk
1 teaspoon fine sea salt
150 g/1¼ cups grated/shredded
   Monterey Jack or other mild,
   semi-hard cheese
150 g/1¾ cups grated/shredded
   medium Cheddar

Serves 6-8

Bring a large saucepan of water to the boil. Add the coarse sea salt, then let the water return to a rolling boil. Add the macaroni, stir well and cook according to the package instructions until very tender. Stir periodically to prevent the macaroni from sticking together. When cooked, drain, rinse well under running water and let drip dry in a colander.

Preheat the grill/broiler to medium.

To make the béchamel sauce, melt the butter in a saucepan. Stir in the flour and cook, stirring constantly, for 1 minute. Pour in the milk in a steady stream, whisking constantly, and continue to whisk for 3–5 minutes until the sauce begins to thicken. Season with the fine sea salt. Remove from the heat and add the cheeses, mixing well with a spoon to incorporate. Taste and adjust the seasoning.

Put the cooked macaroni in a large mixing bowl. Pour over the hot béchamel sauce and mix well. Adjust the seasoning to taste.

Transfer the macaroni mixture to a baking dish and spread evenly. Top with a good grinding of black pepper and sprinkle the breadcrumbs evenly over the top. Grill/broil for about 5–10 minutes until the top is crunchy and golden brown, then serve immediately.

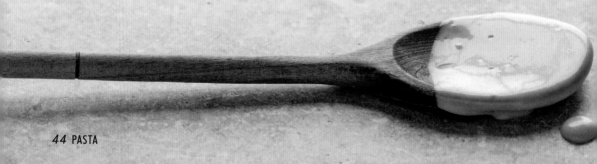

TRUFFLED MAC 'N' CHEESE

handful of coarse sea salt
500 g/1 lb. 2 oz. macaroni
1 quantity béchamel sauce
   (page 44), replacing the
   Monterey Jack and Cheddar
   with 100 g/generous 1 cup
   grated/shredded mature/sharp
   Cheddar, 100 g/scant 1 cup
   grated/shredded Lincolnshire
   Poacher or Gruyère and
   100 g/1¼ cups grated/
   shredded Parmesan
2 tablespoons truffle paste
   or truffle oil
1 preserved truffle, finely
   chopped, reserving 3 slices
   to decorate
50 g/1 cup fresh breadcrumbs
salt and freshly ground
   black pepper

Serves 6-8

IN ORDER TO GET THE BEST RESULTS FROM THIS GOURMET
RECIPE, THE KEY IS TO USE THE HIGHEST QUALITY CHEESES
YOU CAN FIND. CHOOSE A GOOD MATURE/SHARP CHEDDAR,
A PARMESAN REGGIANO AND ANOTHER FLAVOURSOME HARD
CHEESE, SUCH AS LINCOLNSHIRE POACHER OR GRUYÈRE.

Cook the macaroni according to the instructions on page 44.

Preheat the grill/broiler to medium–hot.

Prepare the béchamel sauce according to the instructions on
page 44. Remove from the heat and add the cheeses and
truffle paste or truffle oil, mixing well with a spoon to
incorporate. Taste and adjust the seasoning.

Put the cooked macaroni in a large mixing bowl. Stir in the
chopped truffle, pour over the hot béchamel sauce and mix
well. Taste and adjust the seasoning. Transfer the macaroni
mixture to a baking dish and spread evenly. Top with a good
grinding of black pepper and sprinkle the breadcrumbs
evenly over the top. Decorate with the reserved truffle slices.
Grill/broil for 5–10 minutes until the top is crunchy and
golden brown. Serve immediately.

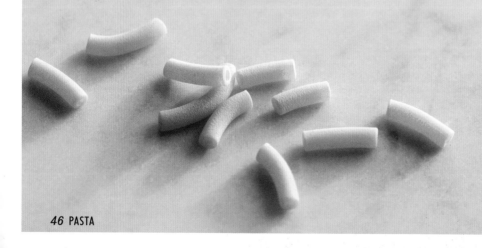

ROASTED ASPARAGUS & PECORINO MAC 'N' CHEESE

ASPARAGUS HAS SUCH A DOMINANT FLAVOUR THAT IT CAN BE DIFFICULT TO FIND A SUITABLE PARTNER. HOWEVER, THE EQUALLY PERVASIVE PECORINO STANDS UP TO THE TASK BEAUTIFULLY.

handful of coarse sea salt
500 g/1 lb. 2 oz. macaroni
800 g/1 lb. 12 oz. asparagus, trimmed
2–3 tablespoons vegetable oil
zest of 1 lemon, finely grated
1 quantity béchamel sauce (page 44), replacing the Monterey Jack and Cheddar with 200 g/2½ cups grated/shredded Pecorino
50 g/1 cup fresh breadcrumbs
salt and freshly ground black pepper

Serves 6-8

Cook the macaroni according to the instructions on page 44.

Preheat the oven to 200°C (400°F) Gas 6.

Arrange the asparagus in a single layer on a baking sheet, sprinkle over the oil and toss to coat lightly. Roast in the preheated oven for about 10–15 minutes until just charred. Remove the asparagus from the oven, cut it in half and put it in a very large bowl. Add the lemon zest, season lightly with salt and set aside.

Preheat the grill/broiler to medium.

Prepare the béchamel sauce according to the instructions on page 44. Remove from the heat and add the cheese, mixing well with a spoon to incorporate. Taste and adjust the seasoning.

Put the cooked macaroni in the bowl with the asparagus. Pour over the hot béchamel sauce and mix well. Taste and adjust the seasoning. Transfer the macaroni mixture to a baking dish and spread evenly. Top with a good grinding of black pepper and sprinkle the breadcrumbs evenly over the top. Grill/broil for 5–10 minutes until the top is crunchy and golden brown. Serve immediately.

PROVENÇAL TOMATO & GOAT'S CHEESE MAC 'N' CHEESE

handful of coarse sea salt

500 g/1 lb. 2 oz. macaroni

500 g/1 lb. cherry tomatoes, halved

small head of garlic, cloves separated but skins left on

few sprigs of fresh thyme, chopped

2–3 tablespoons extra-virgin olive oil

600 ml/2½ cups double/ heavy cream

leaves from a small bunch of fresh basil, thinly sliced

100 g/1¼ cups grated/shredded hard goat's cheese

2 x 60 g/2 oz. Crottin de Chavignol or other mild goat's cheese, ends trimmed and sliced

50 g/1 cup fresh breadcrumbs

salt and freshly ground black pepper

Serves 6-8

A TASTE TRIO THAT SINGS OF MEDITERRANEAN SUNSHINE, THIS MAC 'N' CHEESE MÉLANGE OF THINLY SLICED GOAT'S CHEESE, THYME-SCENTED CHERRY TOMATOES AND FRESH BASIL WILL TRANSPORT YOU STRAIGHT TO THE CÔTE D'AZUR. SERVE WITH A CRISP SIDE SALAD AND A CHILLED BOTTLE OF ROSÉ FROM PROVENCE.

Cook the macaroni according to the instructions on page 44.

Preheat the oven to 190°C (375°F) Gas 5.

Arrange the halved tomatoes and garlic in a single layer on a baking sheet; some skin-side up and some not. Sprinkle over the thyme and oil and toss to coat lightly. Roast in the preheated oven for 15–20 minutes until just charred. Remove the tomatoes and garlic from the oven, slip the garlic cloves out of their skins and chop finely. Set aside. Transfer the tomatoes to a very large bowl and season lightly with salt. Set aside.

Preheat the grill/broiler to medium–hot.

Put the cream in a large saucepan and bring just to the boil, stirring occasionally. Add the basil, chopped garlic and a good pinch of salt, then reduce the heat. Add the grated/shredded goat's cheese and stir well to melt.

Put the cooked macaroni in the bowl with the tomatoes. Pour over the hot cream sauce and mix well. Taste and adjust the seasoning. Transfer the macaroni mixture to a baking dish and spread evenly. Top with a good grinding of black pepper and arrange the Crottin de Chavignol slices on top of the macaroni. Sprinkle with the breadcrumbs and grill/broil for 5–10 minutes until the top is crunchy and golden brown. Serve immediately.

BUTTERNUT SQUASH, CHEDDAR & SAGE MAC 'N' CHEESE

EARTHY SAGE AND SWEET BUTTERNUT SQUASH ARE A MATCH MADE IN HEAVEN — EVEN BETTER TOPPED WITH LASHINGS OF CREAM AND MELTED CHEDDAR. THIS COMFORTING DISH IS PERFECT TO SERVE WHEN THE WEATHER TURNS COLDER.

handful of coarse sea salt
500 g/1lb. 2 oz. macaroni
1 large butternut squash
    (1 kg/2 lb. 4 oz.), skinned,
    deseeded and cubed
3 tablespoons vegetable oil
30 g/2 tablespoons butter
2 shallots, finely chopped
650 ml/2¾ cups double/
    heavy cream
leaves from a few sprigs of
    fresh sage, finely chopped
100 g/1¼ cups grated/shredded
    Padano or Parmesan
100 g/generous 1 cup
    grated/shredded Cheddar
50 g/1 cup fresh breadcrumbs
salt and freshly ground
    black pepper

Serves 6-8

Cook the macaroni according to the instructions on page 44.

Preheat the oven to 200°C (400°F) Gas 6.

Arrange the squash in a single layer on a baking sheet. Sprinkle over 2 tablespoons of the oil and toss to coat lightly. Roast in the preheated oven for 20–25 minutes until just charred. Remove the squash from the oven and put it in a very large bowl. Season lightly with salt and set aside.

Heat the butter and the remaining oil in a large saucepan. Add the shallots and cook over high heat for 2–3 minutes, or until golden, stirring occasionally. Add the cream, sage and a good pinch of salt and bring to the boil, then reduce the heat. Add the cheeses and stir well to melt.

Preheat the grill/broiler to medium–hot.

Put the cooked macaroni in the bowl with the squash. Pour over the hot cream sauce and mix well. Taste and adjust the seasoning. Transfer the macaroni mixture to a baking dish and spread evenly. Top with a good grinding of black pepper and sprinkle the breadcrumbs evenly over the top. Grill/broil for 5–10 minutes until the top is crunchy and golden brown. Serve immediately.

SMOKY MAC 'N' CHEESE
WITH CARAMELIZED ONION

THERE ARE MANY DIFFERENT TYPES OF SMOKED CHEESES, SOME OF WHICH HAVE ACTUALLY BEEN SMOKED AND THOSE THAT SIMPLY HAVE ADDED SMOKE FLAVOURING. THIS NO-FUSS RECIPE WORKS WELL WITH EITHER, SO USE WHATEVER IS READILY AVAILABLE.

handful of coarse sea salt
500 g/1 lb. 2 oz. macaroni
3 tablespoons vegetable oil
750 g/1 lb 10 oz. onions, red and white, halved and thinly sliced
1 heaped teaspoon light brown sugar
3 tablespoons balsamic vinegar
1 quantity béchamel sauce (page 44), replacing the Monterey Jack with 200 g/ scant 2 cups grated/shredded smoked cheese and reducing the quantity of grated/ shredded Cheddar to 100 g/generous 1 cup
50 g/1 cup fresh breadcrumbs
salt and freshly ground black pepper

Serves 6-8

Cook the macaroni according to the instructions on page 44.

Heat the oil in a large frying pan/skillet. Add the onions and cook over high heat for 15–20 minutes until brown and caramelized, stirring occasionally. Add the sugar and vinegar and cook, stirring, until the mixture is almost completely dry; reduce the heat to prevent burning, if necessary. Season with salt and pepper, and set aside.

Preheat the grill/broiler to medium.

Prepare the béchamel sauce according to the instructions on page 44. Remove from the heat and add the cheeses, mixing well with a spoon to incorporate. Taste and adjust the seasoning.

Put the cooked macaroni in a large mixing bowl. Add the onions, pour over the hot béchamel sauce and mix well. Taste and adjust the seasoning. Transfer the macaroni mixture to a baking dish and spread evenly. Top with a good grinding of black pepper and sprinkle the breadcrumbs evenly over the top. Grill/broil for 5–10 minutes until the top is golden brown. Serve immediately.

ARTICHOKE, MUSHROOM & OLIVE PASTA BAKE WITH PROVOLONE

THIS GREAT VEGETARIAN DISH HAS SO MUCH FLAVOUR NO ONE WILL MISS THE MEAT! IT CALLS FOR PROVOLONE, WHICH IS A SMOKED ITALIAN CHEESE, BUT ALMOST ANY CHEESE CAN BE USED, SO EXPERIMENT WITH DIFFERENT TYPES – GRUYÈRE IS GREAT HERE, AS IS SMOKED MOZZARELLA, SOFT GOAT'S CHEESE OR EVEN MATURE/SHARP CHEDDAR.

2–3 tablespoons olive oil
1 onion, finely chopped
½ teaspoon dried oregano
½ teaspoon dried thyme
130 g/2 cups coarsely chopped white mushrooms
4 garlic cloves, crushed
¼ teaspoon chilli/hot red pepper flakes
125 ml/½ cup dry white or red wine
2 x 400-g/14-oz cans chopped tomatoes
400-g/14-oz can artichoke hearts, drained and sliced
50 g/scant ½ cup sliced pitted black olives
pinch of sugar
400 g/14 oz. dried tube pasta, such as penne or rigatoni
150 g/5 oz. provolone, cubed

BÉCHAMEL SAUCE

50 g/3½ tablespoons unsalted butter
35 g/4 tablespoons plain/ all-purpose flour
600 ml/2½ cups hot milk
3–4 tablespoons grated/ shredded Parmesan
salt and ground black pepper

Serves 4

Heat 1 tablespoon of the oil in a large frying pan/skillet. Add the onion and cook over low heat for about 5 minutes, until soft. Stir in the oregano, thyme and mushrooms, and cook for 2–3 minutes more, adding a little more oil if required. Stir in the garlic and chilli/hot red pepper flakes and season with salt. Cook for 1 minute, then add the wine. Cook for 1 minute more, then add the tomatoes, artichokes and olives. Add the sugar, season, stir to combine and simmer for about 15 minutes. Adjust the seasoning to taste.

Preheat the oven to 200°C (400°F) Gas 6.

To prepare the béchamel sauce, melt the butter in a heavy-based saucepan set over low heat. Add the flour and cook, stirring, for 1 minute. Slowly pour in the hot milk, whisking continuously, and simmer until the mixture thickens. Season well. Stir in 2 tablespoons of the Parmesan and set aside.

Cook the pasta according the packet instructions until just al dente. Drain and set aside.

To assemble, spread a small amount of the tomato mixture over the bottom of a baking dish and add 1 tablespoon of the oil. Arrange about one-third of the cooked pasta in a single layer on the bottom. Top with half of the remaining tomato mixture and spread evenly. Cover with another layer of pasta (using half of the remaining amount). Spoon over half of the béchamel and spread evenly. Top with the provolone, spacing the pieces evenly. Spoon the remaining tomato mixture on top. Top with the remaining pasta and béchamel. Sprinkle with the remaining Parmesan. Bake in the preheated oven for about 30–40 minutes, until browned. Serve immediately.

CHEESY RAVIOLI BAKE WITH GRILLED SWEET PEPPERS

2 tablespoons olive oil
1 onion, halved and sliced
225 g/8 oz. frozen mixed grilled
 sweet peppers, or 1 red and
 1 yellow (bell) pepper,
 deseeded and sliced
 (see recipe introduction)
3 garlic cloves, crushed
1 teaspoon dried thyme
¼–½ teaspoon chilli/hot red
 pepper flakes
2 x 400-g/14-oz. cans chopped
 tomatoes
pinch of sugar
large handful of fresh basil
 or flat leaf parsley leaves,
 chopped
500 g/1 lb. 2 oz. small filled
 ravioli or cappeletti
75 g/¾ cup grated/shredded
 Gruyère or medium Cheddar
2 tablespoons grated/shredded
 Parmesan
salt and freshly ground
 black pepper

Serves 4-6

FRESH OR DRIED RAVIOLI BOTH WORK WELL HERE, AND ANY FILLING WILL DO, BUT GOAT'S CHEESE AND PESTO IS AN ESPECIALLY GOOD ONE. FROZEN MIXED GRILLED SWEET PEPPERS ARE FANTASTIC FOR STIRRING INTO ANYTHING THAT NEEDS A QUICK LIFT BUT IF YOU CANNOT FIND ANY, SIMPLY THINLY SLICE A RED AND A YELLOW (BELL) PEPPER AND SWEAT THEM WITH THE ONIONS. THIS IS MEANT TO BE SIMPLE, SO THE INGREDIENT LIST IS SHORT, BUT SOME SLICED MUSHROOMS AND/OR PITTED BLACK OLIVES MAKE A PLEASANT ADDITION IF YOU HAVE SOME.

Preheat the oven to 200°C (400°F) Gas 6.

Heat the oil in a large saucepan. Add the onion and cook over low heat for 3–5 minutes, until soft. Add the peppers, garlic, thyme and chilli/hot red pepper flakes and cook, stirring, for 2–3 minutes. Stir in the tomatoes and sugar, season and simmer, uncovered, for 15 minutes. Taste and adjust the seasoning if necessary. Stir in the basil.

Cook the ravioli according to the packet instructions and drain well.

Tip the cooked ravioli into the sauce and stir gently to coat. Transfer to a lightly greased baking dish, spread evenly and sprinkle both the cheeses over the top.

Bake in the preheated oven for 20–30 minutes, until the cheese is melted and golden. Serve immediately.

SPICY CORN MAC 'N' CHEESE

THE BEST PART OF THIS IS THE WAY THE CRUNCHY SWEETNESS OF THE FRESH CORN KERNELS IS COMPLEMENTED BY THE SMOKY TOASTED CUMIN. DON'T BE TEMPTED TO USE FROZEN OR CANNED CORN IN THIS RECIPE, AS IT SIMPLY WILL NOT TASTE THE SAME.

handful of coarse sea salt
500 g/1 lb. 2 oz. macaroni
4 corn cobs
1½ teaspoons cumin seeds
1 quantity béchamel sauce
   (page 44), increasing the
   quantities of Monterey Jack
   and Cheddar to 200 g/
   1⅔ cups each
1 red chilli/chile, finely diced
   and deseeded, if liked
1 green chilli/chile, finely diced
   and deseeded, if liked
a few sprigs of fresh coriander/
   cilantro, finely chopped
50 g/1 cup fresh breadcrumbs
salt and freshly ground
   black pepper

Serves 6-8

Cook the macaroni according to the instructions on page 44.

Bring a large saucepan of water to the boil. Add the corn cobs and cook for 3 minutes. Drain and let cool slightly, then scrape off the kernels with a sharp knife and set aside.

Heat a small frying pan/skillet until hot but not smoking. Add the cumin seeds and cook until aromatic and beginning to brown. Transfer to a dish to cool, then grind to a powder with a mortar and pestle and set aside.

Preheat the grill/broiler to medium.

Prepare the béchamel sauce according to the instructions on page 44. Remove from the heat and add the cheeses, chillies/chiles and cumin, mixing well with a spoon to incorporate. Taste and adjust the seasoning.

Put the cooked macaroni in a large mixing bowl. Add the corn and coriander/cilantro, pour over the hot béchamel sauce and mix well. Taste and adjust the seasoning. Transfer the macaroni mixture to a baking dish and spread evenly. Top with a good grinding of black pepper and sprinkle the breadcrumbs evenly over the top. Grill/broil for 5–10 minutes until the top is crunchy and golden brown. Serve immediately.

AUBERGINE PARMIGIANA MAC 'N' CHEESE

DRIPPING IN MELTED CHEESE, THIS MAC 'N' CHEESE VERSION OF THE ITALIAN CLASSIC IS ALWAYS A CROWD PLEASER. HERE, THE AUBERGINE/EGGPLANT IS ROASTED, GIVING IT A CRISP TEXTURE.

handful of coarse sea salt
500 g/1 lb. 2 oz. macaroni
4–5 tablespoons vegetable oil
1 large onion, finely chopped
1 teaspoon dried thyme
1 teaspoon dried oregano
1 teaspoon dried rosemary
3 garlic cloves, finely chopped
1 x 400-g/14-oz. can chopped
    tomatoes
1 aubergine/eggplant, sliced
1 quantity béchamel sauce
    (page 44), replacing the
    Monterey Jack and Cheddar
    with 100 g/scant 1 cup
    grated/shredded Fontina
    and 100 g/1¼ cups grated/
    shredded Parmesan
125 g/1 cup shredded mozzarella
leaves from 2–3 sprigs fresh
    basil, coarsely torn
50 g/1 cup fresh breadcrumbs
salt and freshly ground
    black pepper

Serves 6-8

Cook the macaroni according to the instructions on page 44.

Preheat the oven to 200°C (400°F) Gas 6.

Heat 2 tablespoons of the oil in a large sauté pan with a lid. Add the onion and cook over medium heat for 5 minutes until just golden. Stir in the herbs and garlic and cook gently for 1 minute, taking care not to let the garlic burn. Add the tomatoes and 1 teaspoon of salt, and simmer very gently for about 20–30 minutes until very thick.

Arrange the aubergine/eggplant slices in a single layer on a baking sheet and sprinkle over the remaining oil. Roast in the preheated oven for 15–20 minutes until tender and just charred. Remove, season lightly with salt and add to the tomatoes. Simmer gently while you prepare the béchamel sauce.

Preheat the grill/broiler to medium.

Prepare the béchamel sauce according to the instructions on page 44. Remove from the heat and add the Fontina and Parmesan, mixing well with a spoon to incorporate. Taste and adjust the seasoning.

Put the cooked macaroni in a large mixing bowl. Stir in the aubergine/eggplant mixture, pour over the hot béchamel sauce and mix well. Taste and adjust the seasoning. Transfer the macaroni mixture to a baking dish and spread evenly. Top with the mozzarella, the basil leaves and a good grinding of black pepper and sprinkle the breadcrumbs evenly over the top. Grill/broil for 5–10 minutes until the top is crunchy and golden brown. Serve immediately.

BAKED RIGATONI WITH MOZZARELLA

3 tablespoons olive oil
1 small onion, diced
1 carrot, finely diced
2–3 celery sticks, from the inner section, with leaves, diced
1 red, yellow or orange (bell) pepper, deseeded and diced
100 g/1½ cups diced mushrooms
3 garlic cloves, finely chopped
125 ml/½ cup dry white or red wine
½–1 teaspoon chilli/hot red pepper flakes
½ tablespoon fresh thyme leaves or 1 teaspoon dried thyme
large handful of fresh parsley or basil leaves, finely chopped
400-g/14-oz. can chopped tomatoes
700 ml/3 cups passata/ strained tomatoes
pinch of sugar
500 g/1 lb. 2 oz. dried rigatoni
500 g/1 lb. 2 oz. mozzarella, sliced
salt and freshly ground black pepper

Serves 4-6

PUTTING THE MOZZARELLA IN THE MIDDLE AS WELL AS ON TOP OF THIS PASTA BAKE MEANS YOU GET A LOVELY INNER LAYER OF MELTING CHEESE, AS WELL AS A BROWNED TOPPING. BLISSFULLY SIMPLE TO MAKE, OTHER VEGETABLES CAN BE USED HERE ACCORDING TO WHAT'S IN SEASON OR TO HAND – SWEETCORN, BROCCOLI, SPINACH AND COURGETTES/ZUCCHINI WILL ALL WORK NICELY. THE IMPORTANT THING IS TO CHOP ALL THE VEGETABLES INTO DICE OF THE SAME SIZE, TO ALLOW THEM TO NESTLE INSIDE THE PASTA SHAPES.

Heat the oil in a large saucepan, add the onion and cook over low heat for 3–5 minutes, until soft. Add the carrot, celery and (bell) pepper. Season and cook for 2–3 minutes. Stir in the mushrooms and garlic, and cook for 1 minute more. Add the wine and cook for 1 minute more. Stir in the chilli/hot red pepper flakes, thyme, parsley, tomatoes, passata/strained tomatoes and sugar. Season generously and stir. Reduce the heat and simmer, uncovered, for about 20–30 minutes. Taste and adjust the seasoning if necessary.

Meanwhile, cook the pasta according to the packet instructions until al dente. Drain well and set aside.

Preheat the oven to 200°C (400°F) Gas 6.

Combine the cooked pasta and the vegetable sauce, and mix well. Spread half the pasta in the prepared dish evenly. Top with half of the mozzarella. Top with the remaining pasta in an even layer and arrange the remaining mozzarella slices on top.

Bake in the preheated oven for 25–30 minutes, until the cheese melts and bubbles. Serve immediately.

MUSHROOM, TARRAGON & TALEGGIO PASTA BAKE

IT IS THE STRONG AROMA AND FRUITY TANG OF TALEGGIO IN THIS RECIPE THAT TRANSFORMS IT FROM AN ORDINARY MUSHROOM AND CHEESE DISH INTO SOMETHING TRULY SUBLIME. BE SURE TO USE FRESH TARRAGON IF YOU CAN FIND IT.

handful of coarse sea salt
500 g/1 lb. 2 oz. short pasta
300 g/10 oz. Portobello
    mushrooms, stems trimmed
    level with cap
2–3 tablespoons vegetable oil
leaves from a few sprigs of
    fresh parsley, finely chopped
leaves from a few sprigs of
    fresh tarragon, finely chopped
600 ml/2½ cups double/
    heavy cream
100 g/generous 1 cup grated/
    shredded Cheddar
50 g/⅔ cup grated/shredded
    Parmesan
250 g/8 oz. Taleggio, thinly sliced
salt and freshly ground
    black pepper

Serves 6-8

Cook the pasta according to the instructions on page 44.

Preheat the oven to 200°C (400°F) Gas 6.

Arrange the mushrooms in a single layer on a baking sheet, stems up, and brush with the oil. Season lightly with salt, sprinkle over the herbs and roast in the preheated oven for 15–20 minutes until tender. Remove and let cool slightly. Slice the mushrooms and set aside.

Preheat the grill/broiler to medium.

Put the cream in a large saucepan and bring just to the boil, stirring occasionally, then reduce the heat. Add the Cheddar and Parmesan and half the Taleggio, and stir well to melt. Taste and adjust the seasoning.

Put the cooked pasta in a large mixing bowl. Stir in half the sliced mushrooms, pour over the hot cream sauce and mix well. Taste and adjust the seasoning. Transfer the pasta mixture to a baking dish and spread evenly. Top with the remaining mushrooms and Taleggio slices and a good grinding of black pepper. Grill/broil for 5–10 minutes until the top is golden and serve immediately.

SMOKED HADDOCK & SPINACH MAC 'N' CHEESE

CHEDDAR CHEESE, DELICATE SMOKED HADDOCK AND WILTED SPINACH ARE A CLASSIC COMBINATION. THE LIGHT CREAMY SAUCE SPICED WITH NUTMEG REALLY MAKES THESE FLAVOURS SING, RESULTING IN AN IMPRESSIVE DISH INDEED.

a handful of coarse sea salt
500 g/1 lb. 2 oz. macaroni
600 g/1¼ lbs. smoked haddock
   fillets
2 tablespoons vegetable oil
500 g/1 lb. 2 oz. fresh spinach
15 g/1 tablespoon unsalted butter
1 large shallot, finely chopped
600 ml/2½ cups double/
   heavy cream
pinch of grated nutmeg
200 g/2¼ cups grated/shredded
   medium Cheddar
50 g/1 cup fresh breadcrumbs
salt and freshly ground
   black pepper

Serves 6-8

Cook the macaroni according to the instructions on page 44.

Arrange the haddock fillets in a microwaveable dish in a single layer, skin-side down, and pour over just enough water to cover. Cover with clingfilm/plastic wrap and microwave on high for 4–5 minutes, or until the flesh flakes easily. Flake the fish, discard the skin and cooking liquid and remove any bones. Set aside.

Heat 1 tablespoon of the oil in a deep frying pan/skillet. Add half the spinach and cook over high heat, stirring often, until wilted. Season lightly with salt and pepper, then transfer to a chopping board and spread out to cool. Repeat for the remaining spinach, then chop all the spinach coarsely and set aside in a large mixing bowl.

Preheat the grill/broiler to medium–hot.

In the same large frying pan/skillet, melt the butter and heat the remaining oil. Add the shallot and cook over high heat for about 2–3 minutes until just golden, stirring occasionally. Add the cream, nutmeg and a good pinch of salt, and bring just to the boil, then reduce the heat.

Add the haddock and cheese to the spinach in the bowl and pour over the hot cream mixture. Stir well to melt the cheese, then add the macaroni and mix well. Taste and adjust the seasoning.

Transfer the macaroni mixture to a baking dish and spread evenly. Top with a good grinding of black pepper and sprinkle the breadcrumbs evenly over the top. Grill/broil for 5–10 minutes until the top is crunchy and golden brown. Serve immediately.

REBLOCHON, LEEK & BACON PASTA BAKE

THIS DELICIOUS FRENCH-INSPIRED MAC 'N' CHEESE COMBINES THE TRADITIONAL
INGREDIENTS OF THE CLASSIC ALPINE DISH TARTIFLETTE. ITS HEARTY AND ELEGANT
FLAVOURS MAKE IT PERFECT FOR ENTERTAINING.

handful of coarse sea salt
500 g/1 lb. 2 oz. short pasta
3 large leeks (about 500 g/1 lb.
   2 oz.), sliced into rounds
3 tablespoons vegetable oil
200 g/7 oz. bacon lardons
300 ml/1¼ cups double/
   heavy cream
300 g/1¼ cups crème fraîche/
   sour cream
100 g/generous 1 cup grated/
   shredded mild Cheddar or
   Monterey Jack
250 g/9 oz. Reblochon or other
   rich, soft cow's milk cheese
   such as Brie, half finely diced
   and half thinly sliced
50 g/1 cup fresh breadcrumbs
salt and freshly ground
   black pepper

Serves 6-8

Cook the pasta according to the instructions on page 44.

Preheat the oven to 180°C (350°F) Gas 4.

Arrange the leeks in a single layer on a baking sheet. Sprinkle
over 2 tablespoons of the oil and toss to coat lightly. Roast in the
preheated oven for about 15 minutes until tender and just charred.
Remove the leeks from the oven and transfer to a very large bowl.
Season lightly with salt and set aside.

Heat the remaining oil in a sauté pan. Add the bacon and cook over
medium–high heat for 5–10 minutes until well browned. Drain away
the excess fat and add to the leeks in the bowl.

Preheat the grill/broiler to medium–hot.

Combine the cream and crème fraîche/sour cream in a large
saucepan and bring just to the boil, stirring occasionally. Remove
from the heat, add the grated/shredded cheese and diced Reblochon
and stir well to melt.

Put the cooked pasta in the bowl with the leeks. Pour over the hot
cream sauce and mix well. Taste and adjust the seasoning. Transfer
the pasta mixture to a baking dish and spread evenly. Arrange
the remaining Reblochon slices on top, finish with a good grinding
of black pepper and sprinkle the breadcrumbs evenly over the top.
Grill/broil for 5–10 minutes until the top is crunchy and golden
brown. Serve immediately.

PASTA BAKE WITH HOT DOGS, CHEESE, ONIONS & MUSTARD

FOR BEST RESULTS, BE SURE TO USE BOTH GOOD-QUALITY FRANKFURTERS/HOT DOGS AND FLAVOURSOME CHEESE. RED LEICESTER WORKS WELL HERE, BOTH FOR ITS TANGY TASTE AND ORANGE HUE. IF UNAVAILABLE, A STRONG/SHARP CHEDDAR USED IN COMBINATION WITH A MILDER ORANGE-COLOURED HARD CHEESE WILL ALSO WORK.

handful of coarse sea salt
500 g/1 lb. 2 oz. short pasta
2 tablespoons vegetable oil
1 large onion, coarsely chopped
350–400 g/12–14 oz.
   frankfurters/hot dogs
   (about 8–10), sliced into
   bite-size pieces
1 quantity béchamel sauce
   (page 44), replacing the
   Monterey Jack and Cheddar
   with 300 g/3¼ cups grated/
   shredded Red Leicester
2 heaped tablespoons wholegrain
   mustard, plus extra to serve
50 g/1 cup fresh breadcrumbs
salt and freshly ground
   black pepper

Serves 6–8

Cook the pasta according to the instructions on page 44.

Heat the oil in a large frying pan/skillet. Add the onion and cook over high heat for 5–8 minutes until brown and caramelized, stirring occasionally. Season lightly with salt and pepper. Add the frankfurter/hot dog pieces and cook for 2–3 minutes until just browned. Set aside.

Prepare the béchamel sauce according to the instructions on page 44. Remove from the heat and add the cheeses and the mustard, mixing well to incorporate. Taste and adjust the seasoning.

Preheat the grill/broiler to medium–hot.

Put the cooked pasta in a large mixing bowl. Pour over the hot béchamel sauce, stir in the frankfurter/hot dog mixture and mix well. Taste and adjust the seasoning. Transfer the macaroni mixture to a baking dish and spread evenly. Top with a grinding of black pepper and sprinkle the breadcrumbs evenly over the top. Grill/broil for 5–10 minutes until the top is crunchy and golden brown. Serve immediately.

CHORIZO, SWEET PEPPER & MANCHEGO MAC 'N' CHEESE

A COMBINATION OF SPANISH FLAVOURS COME TOGETHER HERE FOR A MAC 'N' CHEESE FIESTA. MANCHEGO IS A SALTY, INTENSELY FLAVOURED SPANISH CHEESE MADE FROM SHEEP'S MILK. IF THIS IS UNAVAILABLE, REPLACE WITH PECORINO OR MORE CHEDDAR.

handful of coarse sea salt
500 g/1 lb. 2 oz. macaroni
2 tablespoons vegetable oil
1 large onion, finely chopped
1 red (bell) pepper, sliced
250 g/8 oz. chorizo, sliced
1 garlic clove, crushed
1 teaspoon dried thyme
1 x 400-g/14-oz. can
   chopped tomatoes
1 quantity béchamel sauce
   (page 44), replacing the
   Monterey Jack with
   150 g/1¼ cups finely grated/
   shredded Manchego and
   increasing the quantity of
   Cheddar to 200 g/2¼ cups
50 g/1 cup fresh breadcrumbs
salt and freshly ground
   black pepper

Serves 6–8

Cook the macaroni according to the instructions on page 44.

Heat the oil in a large sauté pan with a lid. Add the onion and red (bell) pepper and cook over medium heat for about 5 minutes until the onion is just golden. Add the chorizo and cook for 2–3 minutes until browned, stirring occasionally. Stir in the garlic, thyme and ½ teaspoon of fine sea salt and cook gently for 1 minute, taking care not to let the garlic burn. Add the tomatoes and a grinding of black pepper and simmer very gently for 15–30 minutes until the mixture has reduced to a jam-like consistency. Taste and adjust the seasoning, then set aside.

Preheat the grill/broiler to medium.

Prepare the béchamel sauce according to the instructions on page 44. Remove from the heat and add 100g/¾ cup of the Manchego and the Cheddar, mixing well with a spoon to incorporate. Taste and adjust the seasoning.

Put the cooked macaroni in a large mixing bowl. Pour over the hot béchamel sauce, add the chorizo mixture and mix well. Taste and adjust the seasoning.

In a small bowl, toss together the breadcrumbs, the remaining Manchego and a grinding of black pepper. Set aside.

Transfer the macaroni mixture to a baking dish and spread evenly. Top with a good grinding of black pepper and sprinkle the breadcrumb mixture evenly over the top. Grill/broil for 5–10 minutes until the top is crunchy and golden brown. Serve immediately.

HAM HOCK & SMOKED MOZZARELLA PASTA BAKE

THIS SOPHISTICATED TAKE ON THE CLASSIC COMBINATION OF HAM, CHEESE AND PASTA USES SMOKED MOZZARELLA, WHICH WAS MADE TO BE MELTED.

handful of coarse sea salt
500 g/1 lb. 2 oz. pasta
190 g/6½ oz. cooked ham hock, shredded
250 g/9 oz. smoked mozzarella, finely sliced
1 quantity béchamel sauce (page 44), omitting the Monterey Jack and reducing the quantity of Cheddar to 100 g/¾ cup
50 g/1 cup fresh breadcrumbs
salt and freshly ground black pepper

Serves 6-8

Cook the pasta according to the instructions on page 44.

Combine the ham hock and half the mozzarella and mix well. Taste and adjust the seasoning. Set aside.

Preheat the grill/broiler to medium.

Prepare the béchamel sauce according to the instructions on page 44. Remove from the heat and add the cheese, mixing well with a spoon to incorporate. Taste and adjust the seasoning.

Put the cooked pasta in a large mixing bowl. Pour over the hot béchamel sauce and the ham mixture and mix well. Taste and adjust the seasoning.

Transfer the pasta mixture to a baking dish and spread evenly. Top with the remaining mozzarella and a good grinding of black pepper and sprinkle the breadcrumbs evenly over the top. Grill/broil for 5–10 minutes until the top is crunchy and golden brown. Serve immediately.

BBQ CHICKEN MAC 'N' CHEESE

IDEAL FOR HECTIC HOUSEHOLDS, THIS STRAIGHTFORWARD COMBINATION HAS TASTES THAT APPEAL TO ALL GENERATIONS, WITH THE ADDED BONUS OF BEING VERY QUICK TO PREPARE. SERVE WITH CORN, COLESLAW AND A CRISP GREEN SALAD TO GO WITH THE BARBECUE FLAVOURS.

handful of coarse sea salt
500 g/1 lb. 2 oz. macaroni
250 g/4 oz. skinless and boneless
   poached or roasted chicken,
   shredded
250 ml/1 cup barbecue sauce
1 quantity béchamel sauce
   (page 44), omitting the
   Monterey Jack and increasing
   the quantity of Cheddar
   to 200 g/1⅔ cups
250 g/9 oz. mozzarella, half
   shredded and half sliced
50 g/1 cup fresh breadcrumbs
salt and freshly ground
   black pepper

Serves 6–8

Cook the macaroni according to the instructions on page 44.

Put the shredded chicken and the barbecue sauce in a large bowl and mix well. Taste and adjust the seasoning. Set aside.

Preheat the grill/broiler to medium.

Prepare the béchamel sauce according to the instructions on page 44. Remove from the heat and add the Cheddar and shredded mozzarella, mixing well with a spoon to incorporate. Taste and adjust the seasoning.

Put the cooked macaroni in a large mixing bowl. Pour over the hot béchamel sauce, add the chicken mixture and mix well. Taste and adjust the seasoning.

Transfer the macaroni to a baking dish and spread evenly. Top with the sliced mozzarella and a good grinding of black pepper and sprinkle the breadcrumbs evenly over the top. Grill/broil for 5–10 minutes until the top is crunchy and golden brown. Serve immediately.

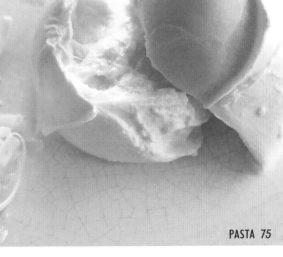

PANCETTA, GORGONZOLA & TOMATO MAC 'N' CHEESE

A STRONGLY-FLAVOURED CHEESE SUCH AS GORGONZOLA PAIRS BEAUTIFULLY WITH A CREAM SAUCE HERE. SMOKY PANCETTA AND A TOMATO REDUCTION BOTH HAVE EQUALLY PUNCHY FLAVOURS THAT MATCH UP TO THE PUNGENT CHEESE WELL.

handful of coarse sea salt
500 g/1 lb. 2 oz. macaroni
2 tablespoons olive oil
1 onion, finely chopped
200 g/7 oz. pancetta, chopped
½ teaspoon dried thyme
1 x 400-g/14-oz. can
   chopped tomatoes
pinch of sugar
600 ml/2½ cups double/
   heavy cream
200 g/1½ cups crumbled
   Gorgonzola
50 g/⅔ cups grated/shredded
   Parmesan
50 g/1 cup fresh breadcrumbs
salt and freshly ground
   black pepper

Serves 6–8

Cook the macaroni according to the instructions on page 44.

Heat the oil in a large frying pan/skillet. Add the onion and cook over high heat for about 5 minutes until just caramelized, stirring occasionally. Stir in the pancetta and thyme, and cook for 2–3 minutes until browned, stirring occasionally. Add the tomatoes, sugar and 1 teaspoon of salt and simmer very gently for 15–30 minutes until the mixture has reduced to a jam-like consistency. Transfer to a large bowl and set aside.

Preheat the grill/broiler to medium–hot.

Put the cream in a large saucepan and bring just to the boil, then reduce the heat. Add the cheeses and stir well to melt.

Put the cooked macaroni in the bowl with the tomato mixture. Pour over the hot cream sauce and mix well. Taste and adjust the seasoning.

Transfer the macaroni mixture to a baking dish and spread evenly. Top with a good grinding of black pepper and sprinkle the breadcrumbs evenly over the top. Grill/broil for about 5–10 minutes until the top is crunchy and golden brown. Serve immediately.

SERRANO HAM, SMOKED PAPRIKA & SPANISH BLUE MAC 'N' CHEESE

THIS TRIO OF FLAVOURS HAS LONG BEEN A FAVOURITE IN SPANISH COOKING, AND THIS PASTA DISH IS YET ANOTHER EXCUSE FOR PUTTING THEM TOGETHER. A ROBUST AND COMFORTING DISH THAT BRINGS THE WARMTH OF THE MEDITERRANEAN TO THE KITCHEN, THIS RECIPE IS PERFECT FOR BRIGHTENING UP COLD WINTER DAYS.

handful of coarse sea salt
500 g/1 lb. 2 oz.macaroni
2–3 tablespoons vegetable oil
1 onion, finely chopped
1 red (bell) pepper, sliced
2 teaspoons sweet smoked
　paprika
100 g/3½ oz. Serrano or other
　cured ham, finely chopped
1 garlic clove, finely chopped
1 x 400-g/14-oz. can
　chopped tomatoes
60 ml/¼ cup red wine
600 ml/2½ cups double/
　heavy cream
200 g/2 ¼ cups grated/shredded
　mild Cheddar cheese or
　Monterey Jack
100 g/¾ cup crumbled
　Spanish blue cheese
50 g/1 cup fresh breadcrumbs
salt and freshly ground
　black pepper

Serves 6-8

Cook the macaroni according to the instructions on page 44.

Heat the oil in a large sauté pan with a lid over medium–high heat. Add the onion and red (bell) pepper, and cook for about 5 minutes until the onion is just golden. Stir in the paprika, ham and garlic and cook gently for 1 minute, taking care not to let the garlic burn. Add the tomatoes and wine, and simmer very gently for 15–30 minutes until the mixture has reduced to a jam-like consistency. Taste and adjust the seasoning.

Preheat the grill/broiler to medium–hot.

Put the cream in a large saucepan and bring just to the boil, then reduce the heat. Add the cheeses and stir well to melt.

Put the cooked macaroni in a large bowl. Pour over the hot cream sauce, add the ham mixture and mix well. Taste and adjust the seasoning.

Transfer the macaroni mixture to a baking dish and spread evenly. Top with a good grinding of black pepper and sprinkle the breadcrumbs evenly over the top. Grill/broil for about 5–10 minutes until the top is crunchy and golden brown. Serve immediately.

GLUTEN-FREE LASAGNE

FOR THE MEAT RAGÙ

1–2 tablespoons olive oil
1 onion, finely chopped
1 garlic clove, finely chopped
1 carrot, peeled, trimmed and
    grated/shredded
750 g/1 lb. 10 oz. lean minced/
    ground beef
200 g/¾ cup passata/strained
    tomatoes
400-g/14-oz. can chopped
    tomatoes
2 bay leaves
70 g/5 tablespoons tomato
    purée/paste
60 ml/¼ cup brandy
250 ml/1 cup red wine
125 ml/½ cup vegetable stock

FOR THE CHEESE SAUCE

50 g/3½ tablespoons butter
1 tablespoon cornflour/cornstarch
500 ml/2 cups warm milk
200 g/2¼ cups grated/shredded
    Cheddar cheese
pinch of grated nutmeg
salt and freshly ground
    black pepper

FOR THE PASTA

115 g/scant 1 cup fine yellow
    cornmeal
60 g/½ cup quinoa flour
3 eggs, beaten
½ teaspoon salt
gluten-free plain/all-purpose
    flour, for dusting

Serves 6-8

THIS DELICIOUS LASAGNE USES A GREAT BASIC GLUTEN-FREE PASTA RECIPE THAT IS VERY USEFUL TO HAVE IN YOUR REPERTOIRE.

Preheat the oven to 180°C (350°F) Gas 4.

For the ragù, heat the oil in a flameproof casserole and cook the onion and garlic until softened. Add the carrot and continue to cook until the carrot starts to soften. Remove the onion, garlic and carrot from the pan and set aside. Add a little more oil to the pan and cook the beef in batches until it is browned. Remove from the pan and drain away any fat, then return the meat to the pan with the onion and carrot mixture. Add the remaining ragù ingredients and bring to the boil. Transfer to the oven and cook for 1 hour until thickened. Remove any excess oil from the top with a spoon, then let cool.

For the cheese sauce, melt the butter in a pan and add the cornflour/cornstarch. Cook for a minute, then add the milk, a little at a time, stirring until you have a smooth sauce. Stir in three-quarters of the cheese. Season with grated nutmeg, salt and pepper, then let cool.

Bring a pan of salted water to the boil. Spread half of the ragù over the base of a baking dish.

For the pasta, sift together the yellow cornmeal and quinoa flour into a mound on a clean work surface. Make a well in the middle, add the eggs and salt, and mix with your fingertips to make a soft dough.

Dust a work surface and rolling pin with flour and cut the pasta dough into quarters. Roll out each quarter very thinly, then cut into rectangular sheets measuring about 15 x 8 cm/6 x 3½ inches.

Cook the first batch of pasta sheets, one at a time, for 2 minutes in the boiling water. Remove each sheet with a slotted spoon and lay it on top of the meat. Repeat to make enough sheets to cover the layer of meat. Top with a thin layer of the cheese sauce. Continue to roll out and cook pasta sheets and layer them on top of the cheese sauce. Spoon the remaining meat ragù on top of the pasta and spread out evenly. Cover with the remaining cheese sauce and top with the reserved cheese. Sprinkle a little nutmeg and black pepper on top, then bake in the preheated oven for 30–40 minutes until the cheese is golden brown on top. Serve straight away.

HAM & EMMENTAL CRÊPES

THESE THIN PANCAKES ARE FILLED WITH A DELICATE BÉCHAMEL SAUCE AND HAM, ROLLED UP AND THEN TOPPED WITH MORE CHEESE, WHICH MELTS WHEN THEY ARE BAKED IN THE OVEN. BE CAREFUL OF THE OOZING CHEESE WHEN PLATING UP!

140 g/1 cup plain/
   all-purpose flour
1 egg and 1 yolk
30 g/2 tablespoons melted butter,
   plus extra butter for cooking
2 teaspoons wholegrain mustard
300 ml/1¼ cups milk
120 g/1 cup wafer-thin ham
150 g/1¼ cups Emmental,
   grated/shredded
salt and freshly ground
   black pepper

FOR THE BÉCHAMEL SAUCE
825 ml/3⅓ cup milk
1 small onion, peeled and
   kept whole
1 teaspoon black peppercorns
2 bay leaves
pinch of grated nutmeg
75 g/5 tablespoons butter
75 g/⅓ cup plain/
   all-purpose flour, sifted

Serves 8

For the sauce, put the milk in a pan set over medium heat. Add the onion, peppercorns, bay leaves and nutmeg, and bring to the boil. Remove from the heat and leave to infuse for 30 minutes. Strain the sauce and discard the onion, bay leaves and peppercorns. In a separate pan, melt the butter until it starts to foam. Tip in all of the flour in one go, remove the pan from the heat and beat the mixture hard until the flour is incorporated and you have a thick paste which leaves the sides of the pan. Reheat the milk and add a little at a time to the flour paste, beating well over the heat as the milk is added. When all the milk is incorporated you should have a smooth white sauce. Season with salt and pepper to taste. Cover and set aside.

To make the crêpe batter, put the flour, egg and egg yolk, butter and mustard in a large mixing bowl. Season well with salt and pepper. Whisking all the time, gradually add the milk until you have a smooth batter. Leave the batter to rest in the fridge for 30 minutes.

Remove the batter from the fridge and stir once. Put a little butter in a frying pan/skillet set over medium heat. Allow the butter to melt and coat the base of the pan, then ladle a spoonful of the batter into the pan and quickly spread it out very thinly. Cook until the top of the pancake is set, then turn over carefully with a spatula and cook on the other side for a further 1–2 minutes until the crêpe is golden brown. Keep warm while you cook the remaining batter.

Preheat the oven to 190°C (375°F) Gas 5.

Spread a generous spoonful of béchamel over each crêpe and top with a few slices of ham. Sprinkle with a little of the cheese and then roll up the crêpe. Place in an ovenproof dish and repeat with all the remaining crêpes. Pour the rest of the béchamel sauce over the pancakes and sprinkle with the remaining cheese. Bake in the preheated oven for 10–15 minutes until the cheese has melted and turns golden brown. Serve immediately.

SEAFOOD LASAGNE

2 tablespoons olive oil
1 onion, chopped
1 celery stick, diced
2 garlic cloves, finely chopped
½ teaspoon chilli/hot red pepper flakes
sprig of fresh thyme
large handful of fresh flat leaf parsley leaves, chopped
400 g/14 oz. mixed seafood (prawns/shrimp, scallops and squid rings)
125 ml/½ cup dry white wine
700 ml/3 cups passata/strained tomatoes
pinch of sugar
8 sheets green lasagne
3 tablespoons grated/ shredded Parmesan
salt and ground black pepper

FOR THE BÉCHAMEL
50 g/3½ tablespoons unsalted butter
40 g/5 tablespoons plain/ all-purpose flour
600 ml/2½ cups hot milk
2 tablespoons grated/shredded Parmesan
3 tablespoons mascarpone
pinch of grated nutmeg
200 g/7 oz. frozen spinach, defrosted

Serves 4-6

A DECADENT VERSION OF A FAMILY FAVOURITE, THIS LASAGNE HAS SHELLFISH, SPINACH AND A BÉCHAMEL MADE EVEN RICHER WITH MASCARPONE. IT MAKES A PLEASANT CHANGE FROM THE CLASSIC MEAT RECIPE AND IS PERFECT FOR SUMMER EATING.

Preheat the oven to 190°C (375°F) Gas 5.

Heat the oil in a large frying pan/skillet. Add the onion and celery and cook over low heat for 3–5 minutes, until soft. Stir in the garlic, chilli/hot red pepper flakes, thyme and parsley, and season generously with salt. Cook, stirring, for 1 minute. Add the seafood and cook, stirring, for 1 minute. Add the wine and cook for 1 minute more. Add the passata/strained tomatoes, season with salt and add the sugar. Stir to blend and simmer gently, uncovered, for 15 minutes.

To make the béchamel, melt the butter in a heavy-based saucepan set over low heat. Stir in the flour and cook, stirring constantly, for 1 minute. Add the hot milk gradually, whisking constantly, and continue whisking gently for 3–5 minutes, until the sauce begins to thicken. Season and stir in the Parmesan and mascarpone until blended. Stir in the nutmeg and spinach.

To assemble, spoon a thin layer of the seafood sauce on the bottom of a baking dish. Return any bits of seafood to the sauce; you just want a thin layer of tomato base for the pasta to sit on. Top with 2 sheets of lasagne. Spread half of the seafood sauce on top, spreading evenly right up to the edges and distribute the seafood evenly on top. Top with 2 sheets of lasagne. Spread half of the béchamel sauce on top, spreading evenly right up to the edges. Continue layering (lasagne, seafood, lasagne, béchamel) and finish with the béchamel.

Sprinkle with the Parmesan and bake in the preheated oven for 25–25 minutes, until just browned. Serve immediately.

CHEESE-TOPPED GNOCCHI BAKE

THIS IS THE ULTIMATE MID-WEEK SUPPER. IT IS QUICK, FILLING AND DELICIOUS. YOU
WON'T BE ABLE TO RESIST THE BUBBLING CHEESY TOP WHEN IT COMES OUT OF THE OVEN.

700 g/1 lb. 9 oz. gnocchi
680 g/2¾ cups passata/
  strained tomatoes
handful of sweetcorn/
  corn kernels
handful of Swiss chard
200 g/scant 2 cups grated/
  shredded mozzarella
handful of breadcrumbs

Serves 4

Preheat the oven to 180°C (350°F) Gas 4.

Cook the gnocchi in a pan of boiling
water as per the packet instructions.
They are ready when they all bob
to the top of the pan.

Drain and put back in the pan
(not over the heat) and stir in
the passata/strained tomatoes,
sweetcorn and chard. Season.
Pour into a baking dish and
sprinkle the mozzarella and
breadcrumbs over the top.

Bake in the preheated oven for
30–40 minutes, or until brown on top.

PASTA, PARMESAN & CHERRY TOMATO PIES

THIS IS A TAKE ON THE CLASSIC SCOTTISH MACARONI PIE OR 'PEH'. THESE ARE DELICIOUS SERVED FRESHLY BAKED OUT OF THE OVEN – ONCE YOU'VE TRIED CHEESY PASTA BAKED IN A PASTRY CASE YOU WILL NEVER LOOK BACK!

900 g/2 lb. store-bought shortcrust pastry dough
110 g/4 oz. dried pasta shapes (such as small rigatoni, fusilli, tubetti or macaroni)
40 g/3 tablespoons butter
2½ tablespoons plain/ all-purpose flour
pinch of cayenne pepper
pinch of English mustard powder
350 ml/1½ cups milk
100 g/generous 1 cup grated/ shredded mature/sharp Cheddar
30 cherry or baby plum tomatoes, halved
50 g/⅔ cup grated/ shredded Parmesan
salt and freshly ground black pepper

6 x 10-cm/4-inch straight-sided ramekins, jars, chef's rings or other small pie moulds

Makes 6

Divide the pastry dough into 6 pieces. On a lightly floured surface, roll out each piece thinly with a rolling pin. Line each mould with a piece of pastry and smooth gently to fit. Don't worry about uneven edges – these will be trimmed off later. Set on a tray and chill for 30 minutes. When firmly set, use a sharp knife to trim the pastry on each one to 5 cm/2 inches deep.

Preheat the oven to 200°C (400°F) Gas 6.

Cook the pasta according to the package instructions. While the pasta is cooking, melt the butter in a pan and add the flour, cayenne pepper and mustard. Cook, stirring, for 1 minute. Remove from the heat. Pour in the milk and whisk in well. Return to the heat and stir until boiling. Simmer, stirring all the time, for 2 minutes.

Drain the pasta and stir into the sauce. Season to taste and stir in the grated/shredded Cheddar. Set aside and leave to cool until tepid.

Spoon the pasta sauce into the pastry cases, leaving enough of a rim of pastry projecting above to hold the tomatoes. Pile the tomato halves over the surface of the pies and sprinkle with the Parmesan. Stand the pies in a shallow baking pan and bake in the preheated oven for 25–30 minutes or until the filling is golden and bubbling and the pastry is cooked through.

VEGETABLES

Gratins • Potato Dishes

SWISS CHARD & GRUYÈRE GRATIN

THIS GRATIN HAS IT ALL – DELICIOUSLY DECADENT CREAM AND MELTED CHEESE AS WELL
AS NUTRITIOUS, IRON-RICH SWISS CHARD. YOU CAN ADD A LITTLE BACON IF YOU WANT
A MEATY HIT ALONGSIDE.

800 g/1¾ lb. Swiss chard
50 g/3½ tablespoons butter
75 g/½ cup plus 1 tablespoon
    plain/all-purpose flour
200 ml/scant 1 cup crème fraîche
300 ml/1¼ cups double/
    heavy cream
pinch of grated nutmeg
50 g/1 cup fresh breadcrumbs
finely grated zest of 1 lemon
    and a good squeeze of juice
50 g/scant ½ cup grated/
    shredded Gruyère
1 tablespoon olive oil
salt and freshly ground
    black pepper

Serves 6

Bring a pan of water to the boil and blanch the chard for
2–3 minutes, then drain and refresh under cold running water.
Squeeze out as much of the water as possible and set aside.

Melt the butter in a pan, add the flour and cook for 1–2 minutes.
Add the crème fraîche, cream and nutmeg. Simmer for about
2–3 minutes. Season.

Preheat the grill/broiler to medium.

Mix the chard and the sauce together and spoon into a large
ovenproof dish. Mix the breadcrumbs with the lemon zest,
cheese and olive oil and sprinkle over the chard and sauce
mixture. Put under the grill/broiler for a couple of minutes until
the gratin is golden brown and bubbling. (If you like, you can
mix the sauce with the chard and leave until ready to cook.
Heat through in a medium oven for 5–10 minutes before
browning under the grill/broiler.)

Serve with a squeeze of lemon juice.

CHARD, ONION, & PARMESAN GRATIN

1 tablespoon olive oil

30 g/2 tablespoons butter

1 onion, roughly chopped

1 teaspoon finely chopped fresh thyme leaves or ½ teaspoon dried thyme

stalks from a large bunch of chard, washed, trimmed, and sliced, plus 4 chard leaves, roughly shredded

1 tablespoon plain/all-purpose flour

150 ml/⅔ cup full-fat/whole milk

1 tablespoon crème fraîche or double/heavy cream (optional)

25 g/⅓ cup freshly grated/ shredded Grana Padano or Parmesan, plus 3 tablespoons for the topping

2 tablespoons fresh breadcrumbs (optional)

salt and freshly ground black pepper

Serves 2 a main meal or 4 as a side

YOU MAY BE TEMPTED TO DISCARD THE FLESHY WHITE CENTRAL RIB OF CHARD LEAVES BUT THEY MAKE A DELICATE-TASTING GRATIN THAT CAN BE SERVED AS A SUMPTUOUS SIDE DISH OR WITH THE ADDITION OF CRUSTY BREAD AND SOME DRESSED SALAD AS A MAIN MEAL.

Heat a non-stick pan, add the oil and 15 g/1 tablespoon of the butter, and tip in the onion. Cover with a lid and cook over low heat for about 5–6 minutes until beginning to soften. Stir in the thyme, then add the chard stalks and cook for another 3–4 minutes. Season.

Preheat the grill/broiler to medium.

Stir the flour into the onion mixture, then add the milk, bring to the boil and simmer until the sauce has thickened. Stir in the chard leaves and cook for 1 minute, then add the crème fraîche and cheese. Tip into an ovenproof dish. Mix the remaining 3 tablespoons of cheese with the breadcrumbs, if using, and scatter over the gratin. Chop the remaining butter into little pieces and dot over the top. Grill/broil until brown and bubbling.

BEEF, COURGETTE & CHEESE GRATIN

IT'S NOT POSSIBLE TO HAVE TOO MANY RECIPES FOR MINCED/GROUND BEEF, AND THIS IS A GREAT ONE. THE GOAT'S CHEESE LIFTS THIS OUT OF THE ORDINARY BUT, AS THE TANGY FLAVOUR IS NOT TO EVERYONE'S TASTE, EXTRA MATURE/SHARP CHEDDAR IS A NICE OPTION IF YOU PREFER. THIS IS IDEAL FOR FEEDING A CROWD AND MAKES A PLEASANT CHANGE FROM LASAGNE.

1 onion, finely chopped
about 125 ml/½ cup olive oil
1 teaspoon dried thyme
1 teaspoon dried oregano
¼ teaspoon chilli/hot red pepper flakes
2 garlic cloves, crushed
125 ml/½ cup dry white or red wine
500 g/1 lb. 2 oz. beef mince/ground beef
400-g/14-oz can chopped tomatoes
pinch of sugar
1.8 kg/4 lb. courgettes/zucchini (about 6), sliced into 1-cm/½-inch rounds
225 g/8 oz. half-fat crème fraîche
60 g/2 oz. soft goat's cheese, crumbled
110 g/1 cup grated/shredded Gruyère or mild Cheddar
1–2 tablespoons milk
salt and freshly ground black pepper

Serves 4–6

In a large frying pan/skillet, combine the onion and 1 tablespoon of the oil. Cook over medium heat for about 3–5 minutes, until soft. Stir in the thyme, oregano, chilli/hot red pepper flakes and garlic, and cook, stirring, for about 1 minute. Add the wine, cook for a further 1 minute, then add the beef. Cook for 5–8 minutes, stirring occasionally, until the beef is browned. Stir in the tomatoes and sugar, and season well. Reduce the heat, cover, and simmer gently for at least 15 minutes.

Preheat the oven to 200°C (400°F) Gas 6.

Meanwhile, prepare the courgettes/zucchini. Line a tray with kitchen paper. Working in batches, heat some of the oil in a large non-stick frying pan/skillet. When hot, add the courgette/zucchini rounds and fry, in a single layer. When just golden, turn and brown the other side. Transfer to the lined tray. Continue until all the courgettes/zucchini are browned.

Stir 2 tablespoons of the crème fraîche into the beef mixture. Put the remaining crème fraîche in a bowl, crumble in the goat's cheese and season with salt and pepper. Mix well. Set aside.

To assemble, arrange one-third of the courgettes/zucchini in an even layer on the bottom of the baking dish. Sprinkle with salt and one-third of the grated cheese. Top with half of the beef mixture, spread evenly. Repeat the courgette/zucchini and beef layer. Finish with a final courgette/zucchini layer. Season with salt, then spread with an even layer of the crème fraîche topping. Sprinkle over the remaining cheese. Bake in the preheated oven for about 30 minutes, until the top is golden brown. Serve with a mixed salad.

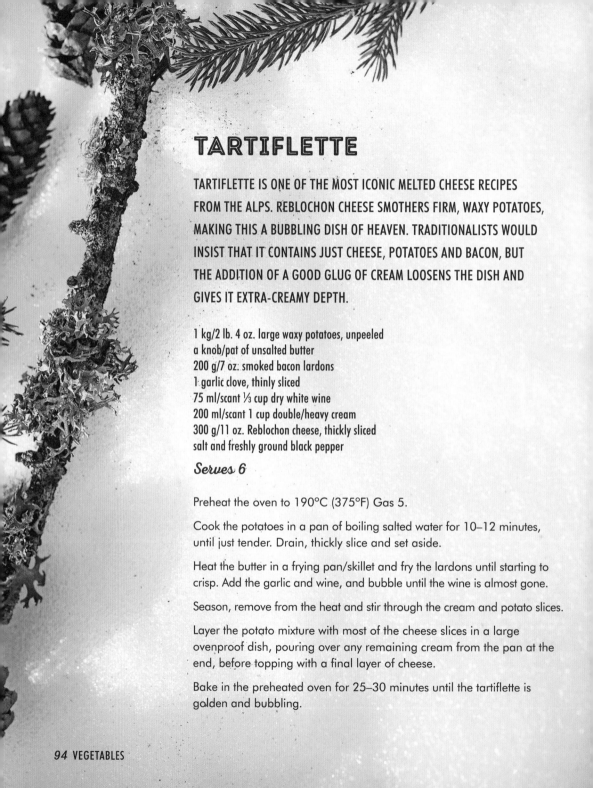

TARTIFLETTE

TARTIFLETTE IS ONE OF THE MOST ICONIC MELTED CHEESE RECIPES FROM THE ALPS. REBLOCHON CHEESE SMOTHERS FIRM, WAXY POTATOES, MAKING THIS A BUBBLING DISH OF HEAVEN. TRADITIONALISTS WOULD INSIST THAT IT CONTAINS JUST CHEESE, POTATOES AND BACON, BUT THE ADDITION OF A GOOD GLUG OF CREAM LOOSENS THE DISH AND GIVES IT EXTRA-CREAMY DEPTH.

1 kg/2 lb. 4 oz. large waxy potatoes, unpeeled
a knob/pat of unsalted butter
200 g/7 oz. smoked bacon lardons
1 garlic clove, thinly sliced
75 ml/scant ⅓ cup dry white wine
200 ml/scant 1 cup double/heavy cream
300 g/11 oz. Reblochon cheese, thickly sliced
salt and freshly ground black pepper

Serves 6

Preheat the oven to 190°C (375°F) Gas 5.

Cook the potatoes in a pan of boiling salted water for 10–12 minutes, until just tender. Drain, thickly slice and set aside.

Heat the butter in a frying pan/skillet and fry the lardons until starting to crisp. Add the garlic and wine, and bubble until the wine is almost gone.

Season, remove from the heat and stir through the cream and potato slices.

Layer the potato mixture with most of the cheese slices in a large ovenproof dish, pouring over any remaining cream from the pan at the end, before topping with a final layer of cheese.

Bake in the preheated oven for 25–30 minutes until the tartiflette is golden and bubbling.

CHICORY GRATIN WITH HAM & BLUE CHEESE

THIS IS A FRENCH RECIPE WHICH TRADITIONALLY CALLS FOR GRUYÈRE CHEESE ONLY, BUT THE BLUE CHEESE USED HERE MAKES IT EVEN BETTER. THERE ARE MANY KINDS OF BLUE CHEESE AND ANY ONE WILL DO FOR THIS DISH. YOU CAN ALSO EXPERIMENT WITH DIFFERENT KINDS OF HAM; CURED HAM WORKS ESPECIALLY WELL, OR, OMIT THE HAM ALTOGETHER FOR AN INDULGENT VEGETARIAN SUPPER. THIS IS AN EXCEPTIONAL WAY TO PREPARE WHAT IS OFTEN THOUGHT OF AS A SALAD-ONLY VEGETABLE. SERVE WITH LOTS OF CRUSTY BREAD OR BOILED POTATOES AND A CRISP GREEN SALAD.

6 chicory (about 90 g/3 oz. each), rinsed and dried
1–2 tablespoons olive oil
12 slices smoked ham
2–3 tablespoons freshly grated/ shredded Gruyère or Parmesan
salt

FOR THE BÉCHAMEL
50 g/3½ tablespoons unsalted butter
35 g/4 tablespoons plain/ all-purpose flour
600 ml/2½ cups hot milk
½ teaspoon salt
½ teaspoon paprika
100 g/scant 1 cup grated/ shredded Gruyère
65 g/generous ½ cup crumbled firm blue cheese

Serves 2

Preheat the oven to 200°C (400°F) Gas 6.

Halve the chicory lengthways. Drizzle with the oil and rub with your hands to coat evenly. Arrange in a single layer on a baking sheet. Sprinkle lightly with salt and drizzle over about 4 tablespoons water. Roast in the preheated oven for about 15 minutes, until just tender when pierced with a knife. Remove from the oven and let cool. Leave the oven on.

Meanwhile, prepare the béchamel. Melt the butter in a heavy-based pan. Stir in the flour and cook, stirring constantly, for 1 minute. Pour in the hot milk gradually, whisking constantly, and continue whisking gently for 3–5 minutes, until the sauce begins to thicken. Season with the salt and paprika, and add both the cheeses. Stir well to combine.

As soon as the chicory are cool enough to handle, carefully wrap each one with a slice of ham and arrange them side-by-side, seam-side down, in the prepared baking dish. Pour over the béchamel, spreading evenly to coat. Sprinkle with the grated cheese and bake in the still hot oven for about 20–30 minutes, until browned and bubbling. Serve immediately.

MUSHROOM, FONTINA, SPINACH & POTATO BAKE

FONTINA IS A DENSE, NUTTY ITALIAN CHEESE THAT MELTS BEAUTIFULLY AND GIVES THE MASHED POTATOES A DELICIOUS GOLDEN CRUST. THIS IS BY NO MEANS A TOKEN VEGETARIAN OPTION – IT IS HEARTY, COMFORTING AND TASTY, AND WILL SATISFY THE HUNGRIEST OF GUESTS. AND LIKE MANY OF THE RECIPES IN THIS CHAPTER, IT CAN BE BAKED AND SERVED IN THE SAME DISH.

1 kg/2 lb. 4 oz. floury potatoes
125 ml/½ cup full-fat/whole milk
pinch of grated nutmeg
125 g/9 tablespoons butter,
    cut into cubes
500 g/1 lb. 2 oz. small chestnut
    mushrooms, left whole and
    stalks removed
4 garlic cloves, roughly chopped
4 spring onions/scallions,
    cut into 2-cm/¾-inch lengths
1 kg/2 lb. 4 oz. spinach, well
    washed and roughly chopped
200 g/7 oz. Fontina, cubed
salt and freshly ground
    black pepper

Serves 4–6

Peel and roughly chop the potatoes. Put them in a large pan of lightly salted boiling water and boil for about 12–15 minutes, until tender but not falling apart. Drain well, return to the warm pan and roughly mash. Add the milk and nutmeg, and season to taste with salt and pepper. Beat with a large wooden spoon or hand-held electric whisk until smooth. Stir through half of the butter, until well combined. Spoon about one-third of the mixture into a baking dish.

Preheat the oven to 180°C (350°F) Gas 4.

Heat half of the remaining butter in a large frying pan/skillet set over medium heat. Add the mushrooms, garlic and spring onions and gently fry for about 10 minutes, until golden. Spoon over the potato mixture in the baking dish.

Heat the remaining butter in the frying pan/skillet and cook the spinach for 5 minutes, stirring often, until just wilted and tender. Season to taste and spoon over the mushrooms in the baking dish.

Spoon the remaining mashed potatoes on top of the spinach and scatter over the Fontina. Bake in the preheated oven for about 30 minutes, until the cheese is bubbly and golden.

GRATIN DE CHOU-FLEUR

THIS IS A SUBLIMELY INDULGENT AND COMFORTING DISH. CAULIFLOWER IS PERFECT PARTNERS WITH MELTED CHEESE AND THIS MAKES A DELICIOUS LOW-CARB ALTERNATIVE TO A TRADITIONAL POTATO GRATIN.

½ cauliflower, cut into florets
2 courgettes/zucchini, thinly sliced
   on an angle
100 g/3½ oz. Brussels sprouts,
   thinly sliced
35 g/2 tablespoons butter
20 g/2½ tablespoons plain/
   all-purpose flour
10 g/2 teaspoons vegetable stock
   powder
500 ml/2 cups full-fat/whole milk
150 g/5½ oz. grated Gruyère
   cheese
1 teaspoon freshly chopped thyme
½ teaspoon freshly grated
   nutmeg
50 g/⅔ cup dried breadcrumbs
salt and freshly ground
   black pepper

baking dish, buttered

Serves 6

Preheat the oven to 190°C (375°F) Gas 5.

Steam the cauliflower in a large pot of boiling water fitted with a steamer basket for 5–7 minutes, until the florets are just tender. Rinse them in cold water, drain, and arrange them in a single layer in the buttered dish. Add the raw sliced courgettes/zucchini and sprouts.

Melt the butter in a large saucepan over a medium heat. Mix together the flour and vegetable stock powder and whisk this into the melted butter until it forms a smooth paste. Continue whisking and cook for about 2 minutes, then gradually add the milk, a little at a time. Add 100 g/3½ oz. of the cheese and stir until melted. Continue whisking and cook until the sauce is heated through, smooth and thickened. Remove from the heat and season with salt, the thyme and nutmeg.

Pour the béchamel sauce over the cauliflower, courgettes/zucchini and sprouts, and gently toss the florets to make sure they are thoroughly coated with the sauce. Bake the gratin, uncovered, in the preheated oven for 15 minutes.

Stir together the remaining grated Gruyère cheese and the breadcrumbs and sprinkle them over the gratin.

Bake it for an additional 10–15 minutes, until the gratin is hot and bubbly and the cheese is melted and browned. Sprinkle the surface of the baked gratin with black pepper and serve hot.

MUSHROOM & POTATO GRATIN WITH GRUYÈRE

A LUXURIOUS TAKE ON A CLASSIC POTATO GRATIN, GIVEN AN UMAMI RICHNESS BY THE ADDITION OF MUSHROOMS AND GRUYÈRE. A GREAT DINNER PARTY DISH, THIS IS AN EXCELLENT ACCOMPANIMENT FOR A RICH BEEF STEW.

25 g/1 oz. dried mushrooms (a mixture of morels, trompette, girolle and porcini)
900 g/2 lbs. waxy potatoes, peeled
300 ml/1¼ cups full fat/whole milk
300 ml/1¼ cups double/heavy cream
sprig of fresh thyme
1 garlic clove, chopped
pinch of grated nutmeg
1 tablespoon olive oil
1 shallot, finely chopped
250 g/8 oz. fresh white/cup mushrooms, thinly sliced
15 g/1 tablespoon butter
150 g/5 oz. Gruyère, thinly sliced
salt and freshly ground black pepper

Serves 6

Soak the dried mushrooms in hot water for 20 minutes; drain and discard the liquid.

Finely slice the potatoes. Bring the milk, double/heavy cream, thyme and garlic to the boil in a pan. Season with salt, freshly ground black pepper and nutmeg. Add the potato slices and simmer for 10 minutes.

Preheat the oven to 180°C (350°F) Gas 4.

Meanwhile, heat the olive oil in a frying pan/skillet. Add the shallot and fry over low heat, stirring, for 2 minutes. Add the sliced mushrooms. Increase the heat to high and fry for a further 3 minutes, stirring, until the mushrooms are lightly browned. Add the soaked dried mushrooms. Season with salt and freshly ground black pepper.

In a shallow, ovenproof dish, arrange one-third of the creamy potato mixture in a layer at the bottom of the dish. Top with half of the Gruyère slices and then a layer of the mushroom mixture. Repeat the layers, then finish with the last of the potato mixture. Dot the surface with butter. Bake in the preheated oven for 50–60 minutes, until golden-brown. Serve hot from the oven.

BUTTERNUT SQUASH, SWEETCORN & BREAD PUDDING WITH CHEESE & CHIVES

THIS SAVOURY BREAD PUDDING HAS THE ADDITION OF A FEW VEGETABLES, WHICH MAKES IT MORE OF A MEAL. THE SWEETNESS OF THE BUTTERNUT SQUASH AND SWEETCORN GO WELL WITH THE CREAMY, CHEESY BREAD PUDDING PART. IN PLACE OF THE BAGUETTE, YOU COULD SAVE UP THE ENDS FROM SLICED LOAVES. ANY KIND OF CHEESE CAN BE USED HERE, AS CAN A COMBINATION OF CHEESES, SO IT'S A GOOD WAY TO USE UP ANY ODDS AND ENDS YOU HAVE LURKING IN THE FRIDGE.

1 tablespoon olive oil
1 large onion, halved and thinly sliced
375 ml/1⅔ cups milk
225 ml/scant 1 cup single/light cream
3 eggs, beaten
small bunch of fresh chives, snipped
leaves from a small bunch of fresh parsley, finely chopped
1 baguette, cut into 5-mm/¼-inch slices
300 g/generous 2 cups sweetcorn kernels, canned or frozen
about 500 g/1 lb. 2 oz. peeled and sliced butternut squash
100 g/generous 1 cup grated/shredded mature/sharp Cheddar
salt and freshly ground black pepper

Serves 4-6

Preheat the oven to 190°C (375°F) Gas 5.

Heat the oil in a large frying pan/skillet. Add the onion and cook over low heat for 3–5 minutes until softened. Season lightly and set aside.

Combine the milk, cream and eggs in a small bowl and whisk to combine. Season with 1½ teaspoons salt. Add the chives and parsley, mix well and set aside.

Arrange half the baguette slices in a greased baking dish in a single layer; you may need to tear some to cover all the space. Put half of the onion slices on top, then scatter over half of the sweetcorn. Arrange half of the squash slices evenly on top and sprinkle with half of the cheese. Repeat one more time (bread, onion, sweetcorn, squash, cheese). Stir the milk mixture and pour it evenly all over the pudding.

Cover tightly with foil and bake in the preheated oven for 20 minutes. Remove the foil and continue baking for about 30–40 minutes, until golden. Serve immediately.

ROOT VEGETABLE GRATIN

THIS IS A RUSTIC, HEARTY DISH, AND THE MELTED CHEESE IT IS TOPPED WITH MAKES IT COMFORTING AND SATISFYING IN ADDITION TO THE NOURISHMENT YOU GET FROM THE MANY DIFFERENT TYPES OF VEGETABLES. IT IS SIMPLE TO PREPARE, THE MOST TIME CONSUMING PART IS CHOPPING THE VEGETABLES, BUT THEN YOU CAN PUT IT IN THE OVEN AND LET THAT WORK ITS MAGIC WHILE YOU RELAX AND WAIT FOR YOUR MEAL.

3 small turnips (about 375 g/13 oz.), peeled, halved and very thinly sliced
½ a celeriac (about 325 g/11 oz.), peeled, halved and very thinly sliced
½ a swede (about 450 g/1 lb.), peeled, halved and very thinly sliced
650 g/1 lb. 7 oz. waxy potatoes, peeled, halved and very thinly sliced
225 ml/scant 1 cup double/heavy cream
100 g/⅓ cup crème fraîche
250 ml/1 cup milk
125 g/scant 1½ cups grated/shredded/Gruyère or medium Cheddar
salt and freshly ground black pepper

Serves 4-6

Preheat the oven to 200°C (400°F) Gas 6.

Put all the vegetable slices in a large bowl and toss gently to combine. Set aside.

Combine the cream, crème fraîche and milk in a small saucepan and heat just to melt the crème fraîche. Stir well, season with salt and pepper.

Arrange half of the vegetables slices in a buttered baking dish. Sprinkle with a little salt and one-third of the cheese. Pour over one-third of the cream mixture.

Top with the rest of the vegetable slices, the remaining cheese and a sprinkle of salt. Pour over the remaining cream mixture and bake in the preheated oven for 1–1½ hours, until browned on top. Serve immediately.

COURGETTE GRATIN WITH FRESH HERBS & GOAT'S CHEESE

THIS GRATIN INCLUDES A TOPPING OF TANGY GOAT'S CHEESE. IF YOU GROW YOUR OWN HERBS, ADD WHATEVER IS ON OFFER: SAVORY, MAJORAM, OREGANO OR ANY OTHER SOFT-LEAVED HERB, THE MORE THE MERRIER. THIS IS PERFECT, SIMPLY SERVED WITH A MIXED SALAD OF LETTUCE AND RIPE TOMATOES AND A BIG BASKET OF FRESH CRUSTY BREAD.

250 ml/1 cup double/heavy cream
leaves from a small bunch
    of fresh flat leaf parsley,
    finely chopped
small bunch of fresh chives,
    snipped
pinch of grated nutmeg
75 g/¾ cup grated/shredded
    Gruyère
1.5 kg/3¾ lb. courgettes/zucchini,
    very thinly sliced
150 g/5 oz. soft goat's cheese
salt and freshly ground
    black pepper

Serves 4

Preheat the oven to 190°C (375°F) Gas 5.

Put the cream, parsley, chives, nutmeg, salt and pepper in a small bowl and whisk together. Add half the Gruyère.

Arrange half the courgette/zucchini slices in a buttered baking dish, sprinkle with the remaining Gruyère and season with a little salt. Top with the remaining courgette/zucchini slices, season again and pour over the cream mixture. Crumble the goat's cheese over the top.

Bake in the preheated oven for about 35–45 minutes, until browned. Serve immediately with a mixed salad and plenty of crusty bread.

NOTE If preferred, you can make the gratin in 4 individual dishes, simply reduce the cooking time by about 5–10 minutes.

SALMON, BROCCOLI &
PARMESAN GRATIN WITH PESTO

IF YOU DON'T HAVE TIME TO MAKE PESTO, FEEL FREE TO USE A GOOD-QUALITY STORE-BOUGHT
FRESH ONE. ALTERNATIVELY, YOU CAN REPLACE IT WITH SOME CHOPPED FRESH PARSLEY, LOTS
OF FRESHLY GROUND BLACK PEPPER AND 1 TABLESPOON OF GRATED LEMON ZEST FOR AN
EQUALLY DELICIOUS BUT DIFFERENT TASTE.

975 g/1 lb. 14 oz. waxy
    potatoes, peeled
large head of broccoli
    (about 480 g/1 lb. 1 oz.),
    separated into florets
400 g/14 oz. boneless,
    skinless salmon fillet
1 tablespoon olive oil
20 g/generous ⅓ cup fresh
    breadcrumbs
4 tablespoons freshly grated/
    shredded Parmesan
250 ml/1 cup single/light cream
2 tablespoons fresh pesto
4 tablespoons milk
30–40 g/2–3 tablespoons butter,
    cut into small pieces
salt and freshly ground
    black pepper

Serves 4-6

Preheat the oven to 200°C (400°F) Gas 6.

Put the potatoes in a large pan and add sufficient cold water to
cover. Parboil until almost tender when pierced with a knife. Drain.
When cool enough to handle, slice into 3-mm/⅛-inch thick rounds.

Bring another pan of water to the boil. Add the broccoli and a pinch
of salt and cook for 3–4 minutes, until just tender. Drain and let cool.
Cut into bite-sized pieces and set aside.

Rub the salmon fillets with the oil and place on a sheet of foil,
turned up at the sides to catch any juices, and put it on a baking
sheet. Sprinkle with a little salt. Bake in the preheated oven for about
10–15 minutes, until cooked through. Let cool, then flake, removing
any small bones and set aside.

In a small bowl, mix together the breadcrumbs and 2 tablespoons
of the Parmesan. Season well and set aside. In another bowl, stir
together the cream and pesto. Season well and set aside.

To assemble, arrange the potato slices on the bottom of the prepared
baking dish in an even layer, sprinkle with salt, the remaining
Parmesan and drizzle with the milk. Arrange the broccoli in an even
layer on top of the potatoes and season lightly. Top with the cooked
salmon in an even layer.

Pour over the pesto and cream mixture. Sprinkle the breadcrumb
mixture over the top and dot with the butter. Bake in the preheated
oven for 25–30 minutes, until just browned and crisp on top.
Serve immediately.

CHEESY POLENTA & ROASTED VEGETABLE PIE

POLENTA IS CLASSIC ITALIAN CORNMEAL, WHICH IS COOKED INTO A KIND OF PORRIDGE. FOR THIS RECIPE YOU NEED THE QUICK-COOK VERSION, AS IT CAN BE PREPARED VERY SPEEDILY. IT IS USED HERE TO COVER OVEN-ROASTED VEGETABLES AND TOPPED WITH MELTING MOZZARELLA, TO MAKE A COMFORTING AND NUTRITIOUS PIE.

2 small courgettes/zucchini
1 red (bell) pepper
1 yellow (bell) pepper
300 g/10 oz. broccoli, sliced into long thin 'trees'
1 red onion, sliced into thick rings
2–3 tablespoons extra-virgin olive oil
200 g/1⅓ cups quick-cook polenta/cornmeal
1 tablespoon butter
80 g/scant 1 cup grated/shredded Cheddar
125-g/4½-oz. mozzarella ball, sliced
salt

Makes 6–8 servings

Preheat the oven to 200°C (400°F) Gas 6.

Cut the courgettes/zucchini in half widthwise, then halve lengthwise and cut into long thin fingers. Deseed the (bell) peppers, then cut into thick slices. Spread the vegetables in a single layer on a baking sheet and add the broccoli and onion. Drizzle over the oil and toss to coat. Season lightly with salt and roast in the preheated oven for about 10–20 minutes, until just tender and lightly browned. You may need to roast in batches, depending on the size of your vegetables. The broccoli may cook faster. Check after 15 minutes and remove it if necessary, continue cooking the other vegetables. Remove from the oven and transfer to the prepared dish.

Put 800 ml/3¼ cups water in a large pan, season lightly and add the polenta in a stream. Cook, whisking constantly, until thick. Take care as polenta can bubble up a bit ferociously.

When thick, lower the heat and continue cooking, stirring constantly, for 5 minutes more.

Remove from the heat, stir in the butter and Cheddar. Pour over the vegetables in the dish and spread out evenly with a spatula. Arrange the mozzarella slices on top and bake in the preheated oven for about 25 minutes, until browned and bubbling. Serve hot.

VEGETABLE ENCHILADAS

2 tablespoons olive oil

450 g/1 lb. courgettes/zucchini, diced

1 red onion, diced

150 g/generous 1 cup sweetcorn kernels, canned or frozen

½ fresh red or green chilli/chile, halved, deseeded and sliced

1 teaspoon ground cumin

400-g/14-oz. can black beans, drained

large handful of fresh coriander/cilantro leaves, chopped

8 corn tortillas

250 g/2¾ cups grated/shredded mild Cheddar

sour cream, to serve

FOR THE SAUCE

1 onion, coarsely chopped

2 garlic cloves

2 tablespoons olive oil

1–2 teaspoons chilli/hot red pepper flakes, to taste

½ teaspoon Spanish hot smoked paprika or cayenne pepper

1 teaspoon ground cumin

1 teaspoon dried oregano

700 ml/3 cups passata/strained tomatoes

1 vegetable stock/bouillon cube dissolved in 375 ml/1⅔ cups hot water

salt and freshly ground black pepper

Serves 4

THESE MOUTH-WATERING HOME-MADE ENCHILADAS ARE BOTH STUFFED WITH AND TOPPED WITH MELTED CHEESE. DELICIOUS!

Preheat the oven to 200°C (400°F) Gas 6.

To make the sauce, put the onion and garlic in a food processor and pulse until finely chopped. Transfer to a large frying pan/skillet. Add the oil and cook over low heat, stirring, for 3–5 minutes, until just soft. Stir in the chilli/hot red pepper flakes, paprika, cumin and oregano and add salt to taste. Cook, stirring, for 2 minutes. Add the passata/strained tomatoes and stock, and simmer gently, uncovered, for at least 15 minutes. Let cool slightly.

Meanwhile, make the filling. Heat the oil in a large saucepan, add the courgettes/zucchini and onion, and cook over low heat for 5–8 minutes, until just tender. Stir in the sweetcorn, chilli/chile, cumin and beans, and season to taste. Remove from the heat and stir in the coriander/cilantro, reserving some to garnish.

To assemble, warm the tortillas according to the packet instructions. Coat the bottom of a baking dish with a layer of the tomato sauce. Working one at a time, dab a tortilla gently in the warm sauce in the pan, just to coat the bottom side, then turn over to coat the other side. (If you use tongs for this, be careful not to tear the tortillas.)

Transfer the coated tortilla to a plate and fill with a large spoonful of filling and a handful of grated cheese, then fold the tortilla over to enclose the filling and transfer it in a baking dish, seam-side down. Continue until all the tortillas have been filled. Spoon the remaining sauce over the tortillas, concentrating on the ends as these tend to dry out. Sprinkle the remaining cheese down the centre.

Bake in the preheated oven for 15–20 minutes, until the cheese has melted. Sprinkle with the reserved coriander/cilantro and serve with sour cream on the side.

COURGETTE & FETA GRIDDLE CAKES

THESE PANCAKES ARE QUICK AND EASY TO PREPARE AND MAKE A GREAT ACCOMPANIMENT TO
SOUPS AS AN ALTERNATIVE TO BREAD. THE FETA CHEESE MELTS WHEN COOKED, GIVING THEM
A LOVELY SOFT TEXTURE. THEY ARE MADE WITH RAW COURGETTE/ZUCCHINI, BUT IF YOU PREFER,
YOU CAN FRY THEM IN A LITTLE OLIVE OIL BEFORE ADDING TO THE PANCAKE BATTER, MAKING
SURE THAT YOU DRAIN THE COURGETTE/ZUCCHINI OF ITS COOKING JUICES AND COOL FIRST.

150 g/generous 1 cup
   self-raising/rising flour, sifted
2 eggs, separated
250 ml/1 cup milk
70 g/5 tablespoons butter,
   melted and cooled,
   plus extra for frying
1 teaspoon baking powder
1 large courgette/zucchini,
   grated/shredded
   (approx. 200 g/2½ cups)
200 g/1½ cups feta cheese,
   crumbled
1 tablespoon freshly chopped
   mint
salt and freshly ground
   black pepper, to taste

Makes 10

Put the flour, egg yolks, milk, melted butter and baking powder in
a large mixing bowl and whisk together. Season well with salt and
pepper and mix again until you have a smooth batter.

In a separate bowl, whisk the egg whites to stiff peaks. Gently fold
the whisked egg whites into the batter mixture using a spatula.
Cover and put in the refrigerator to rest for 30 minutes.

When you are ready to serve, remove the batter mixture from the
refrigerator and stir gently. Add the grated courgette/zucchini to
the batter with the feta cheese and mint.

Put a little butter in a large frying pan/skillet set over medium heat.
Allow the butter to melt and coat the base of the pan, then ladle
small amounts of the rested batter into the pan, leaving a little space
between each. Cook until the underside of each pancake is golden
brown and a few bubbles start to appear on the top; about 2–3
minutes. Turn the pancake over using a spatula and cook on the
other side until golden brown. It is important that they cook all the
way through to ensure that the middle of your pancakes are not
soggy. Serve immediately.

SQUASH & GOAT'S CHEESE PANCAKES

PERFECT FOR LUNCH, THESE PANCAKES ARE TOPPED WITH SOUR CREAM OR CRÈME FRAÎCHE AND DRIZZLED WITH DELICIOUS PUMPKIN SEED OIL. USE A MILD, CREAMY GOAT'S CHEESE SO THAT THE FLAVOUR IS NOT OVERPOWERING. TRY USING HALEN MÔN SEA SALT (AVAILABLE ONLINE), WHICH IS FRAGRANCED WITH CUMIN, NUTMEG, PAPRIKA, CLOVES AND CINNAMON.

1 butternut squash, peeled
  and seeds removed
  (670 g/2½ lb), diced
2 tablespoons olive oil
1 teaspoon black onion seeds
pinch of spiced sea salt
  or regular sea salt
4–5 curry leaves, crushed
1–2 garlic cloves, skins on
200 g/1⅔ cups self-raising/
  rising flour, sifted
2 teaspoons baking powder
1 egg
300 ml/1¼ cups milk
3 tablespoons melted butter,
  plus extra for greasing
125 g/1 cup soft goat's cheese
sour cream, to serve
a bunch of Greek basil leaves,
  to garnish
pumpkin seed oil, to drizzle
salt and freshly ground
  black pepper, to taste

Serves 4

Preheat the oven to 180°C (350°F) Gas 4.

Put the diced butternut squash in a greased roasting pan. Drizzle with the olive oil and sprinkle over the onion seeds, salt and curry leaves. Stir so that the squash is well coated in the oil and spices, then add the garlic cloves. Roast in the preheated oven for 35–45 minutes until the squash is soft and starts to caramelize at the edges. Leave to cool.

To make the pancake batter, put the flour, baking powder, egg and milk in a large mixing bowl and whisk together. Season with salt and pepper. Add the melted butter and whisk again. The batter should have a smooth, dropping consistency. Add about two-thirds of the butternut squash to the batter and set aside.

Remove the skins from the garlic cloves and mash to a paste using a fork. Whisk into the batter then crumble in the goat's cheese. Mix together gently. Cover and put in the refrigerator to rest for 30 minutes.

Put a little butter in a large frying pan/skillet set over a medium heat. Allow the butter to melt and coat the base of the pan, then ladle spoonfuls of the rested batter into the pan, leaving a little space between each.

Cook until the underside of each pancake is golden brown and a few bubbles start to appear on the top – this will take about 2–3 minutes. Turn the pancake over using a spatula and cook on the other side until golden brown.

Serve the pancakes, topped with a spoonful of sour cream, a few sprigs of basil and the reserved butternut squash. Drizzle with pumpkin seed oil and sprinkle with freshly ground black pepper.

DIPS & SOUPS

Hot Dips • Fondues • Soups

HAWAIIAN-STYLE CHEESE, BACON & PINEAPPLE DIP

THIS DECADENT HOT DIP IS MADE WITH GOOEY MELTED CHEESE, PINEAPPLE AND SALTY PANCETTA. YOU CAN REPLACE THE PANCETTA WITH READY-COOKED HAM OR FRIED BACON LARDONS IF YOU PREFER. OR, IF PEPPERONI PIZZA IS YOUR FAVOURITE, TRY SWAPPING THE PANCETTA FOR PEPPERONI SLICES. FRESH PINEAPPLE HAS LOTS OF FLAVOUR, BUT CANNED PINEAPPLE IS ALSO FINE TO USE AND IS QUICKER TO PREPARE.

100 g/3½ oz. pancetta
　rashers/slices
4 slices of fresh pineapple
　or 4 canned pineapple rings
250 g/9 oz. cream cheese
125 ml/½ cup your favourite
　Thousand Island dressing
1 tablespoon sun-dried
　tomato purée/paste
100 g/generous 1 cup
　grated/shredded Red Leicester
　or Colby cheese
salt and freshly ground
　black pepper
tortilla chips or crusty bread,
　to serve

Serves 6-8

Preheat the oven to 180°C (350°F) Gas 4.

Chop the strips of pancetta into 2.5-cm/1-inch pieces and put in a roasting pan. If using a fresh pineapple, remove the skin, eyes and hard core, then chop into small pieces. If using canned pineapple, chop the rings into small pieces. Add the pineapple to the roasting pan and bake in the preheated oven for 10 minutes. Remove from the oven and leave to cool slightly. Leave the oven on.

Put the cream cheese in a mixing bowl. Add the Thousand Island dressing and tomato purée/paste and whisk together until smooth. Stir in the grated/shredded cheese, cooled pancetta and pineapple pieces, and season with salt and pepper. Bake in the still hot oven for 20–25 minutes until golden brown on top. Leave to cool slightly for about 10 minutes, then serve warm with tortilla chips or crusty bread for dipping.

VARIATION For a Hawaiian 'pizza' dip, try using pepperoni slices instead of the pancetta and arrange them on top of the dip as you would with a pizza. This cute novelty presentation is guaranteed to appeal to kids!

HOT PHILLY CHEESESTEAK DIP

THIS RECIPE IS INSPIRED BY ONE OF THE MOST POPULAR STEAK RECIPES IN AMERICA — A PHILLY CHEESESTEAK — A STEAK SANDWICH MADE WITH THIN SLICES OF BEEF, TOPPED WITH MELTING CHEESE. DIP IN TORTILLA CHIPS OR CRUSTY BREAD WHILE WATCHING THE SUPER BOWL.

1 green (bell) pepper
1 onion
1 tablespoon olive oil
1 teaspoon balsamic glaze
or vinegar
1 teaspoon caster/
granulated white sugar
6 slices roast beef
250 g/9 oz. cream cheese
125 ml/½ cup your favourite
ranch salad dressing
1 tablespoon creamed
horseradish
100 g/generous 1 cup
grated/shredded Provolone
or Cheddar
salt and freshly ground
black pepper
tortilla chips or crusty bread,
to serve

Serves 6-8

Preheat the oven to 180°C (350°F) Gas 4.

Cut away the top of the (bell) pepper and discard. Cut the pepper in half, remove all of the seeds, then cut into small chunks about 1 cm/⅜ inch in diameter. Peel and finely chop the onion. Put the peppers and onion in a large frying pan/skillet with the olive oil and fry over gentle heat until the onion and pepper are soft and the onion starts to caramelize. Drizzle with the balsamic glaze, sprinkle over the caster/granulated sugar, season with salt and pepper and fry for a few more minutes.

Cut the roast beef into small pieces and add to the pan. Cook for a minute or so, so that the meat absorbs the flavours from the pan. Remove from the heat and leave to cool for a few minutes.

In a mixing bowl, whisk together the cream cheese, ranch dressing and creamed horseradish. Fold the grated cheese into the mixture with the beef and vegetables.

Bake in the preheated oven for 20–25 minutes until the cheese has melted and the top of the dip has started to turn light golden brown. Leave to cool for about 10 minutes before serving, as the dip should be served warm and not hot. Serve with tortilla chips or slices of crusty bread for dipping. Delicious!

VARIATION To make a spicy version, fold in some finely chopped jarred jalapeños with the beef before baking.

MARYLAND CRAB DIP

WITH BOTH RICH AND CREAMY CHEESE AND A MILD SPICY HEAT, THIS DIP IS A DELICIOUS CLASSIC. FOR A TWIST, FOLD IN CHOPPED LOBSTER OR PRAWNS/SHRIMP IN PLACE OF THE CRAB.

150 g/5½ oz. cream cheese
125 ml/½ cup buttermilk
2 tablespoons mayonnaise
1 tablespoon hot chilli/chili sauce (such as Frank's)
freshly ground black pepper
freshly squeezed juice of 1 lemon
120 g/scant 1½ cups grated/shredded Cheddar or Provolone
100 g/3½ oz. white or brown crabmeat
a pinch of ground chilli/chili pepper
3 tablespoons panko breadcrumbs
celery sticks, to serve

Serves 6-8

Preheat the oven to 180°C (350°F) Gas 4.

Place the cream cheese, buttermilk and mayonnaise in a bowl and whisk together until smooth. Add the hot sauce, a grind of black pepper and lemon juice, and whisk to combine. Divide the grated cheese into ⅔ and ⅓. Add the larger portion to the mix with the crabmeat and chilli/chili pepper, and fold together gently until mixed. Spoon into an ovenproof bowl. Cover the top with the remaining cheese and sprinkle over the panko breadcrumbs.

Bake in the preheated oven for 20–25 minutes until the cheese on top is golden brown. Remove from the oven and leave to cool for 10 minutes before serving with celery sticks and tortilla chips for dipping.

HOT BUFFALO CHICKEN & MELTED CHEESE DIP

THIS DIP HAS THE TASTE OF HOT BUFFALO WINGS BUT WITHOUT THE BOTHER OF GETTING MESSY FINGERS EATING ACTUAL WINGS. HOT SAUCES VARY IN FIERCENESS SO PLEASE DO ADD GRADUALLY.

300 g/10½ oz. cream cheese
170 ml/¾ cup ranch salad dressing
125 ml/½ cup red hot chilli sauce (such as Frank's)
150 g/1¾ cups grated/shredded Cheddar
200 g/7 oz. cooked chicken breast
freshly ground black pepper
tortilla chips, to serve

Serves 6-8

Preheat the oven to 180°C (350°F) Gas 4.

Put the cream cheese, ranch dressing and hot sauce in a bowl and whisk together until smooth. Stir in the grated cheese. Remove any skin from the chicken breasts and discard, then chop into small pieces and stir into the sauce. Season with cracked black pepper and taste. Add a little salt if you wish, but there should be sufficient salt from the dressing and hot sauce.

Bake in the preheated oven for 25–30 minutes until the top of the dip starts to turn golden. Remove from the heat and leave to cool for a short while then serve warm with tortilla chips.

VARIATION To make a version suitable for vegetarians, simply use a vegetarian cheese and replace the cooked chicken breast with butter/lima beans or small florets of steamed or boiled cauliflower.

TRADITIONAL CHEESE FONDUE

1 fat garlic clove, halved
2 teaspoons cornflour/cornstarch
400 ml/1¾ cups hoppy lager beer
800 g/7 cups grated/shredded
  mixture of Swiss or French
  Alpine cheeses, such as Gruyère
  or Comté, Vacherin
  Fribourgeois, good-quality
  Emmental and Beaufort —
  choose two or three cheeses
1–2 teaspoons whisky, to taste
1 large loaf of slightly stale
  country white bread,
  cut into cubes
gherkins, pickled silverskin
  onions and charcuterie,
  to serve

Serves 6–8

MADE WITH A MELANGE OF CHEESES, A TRUE SWISS FONDUE IS A MIXTURE OF GRUYÈRE AND VACHERIN FRIBOURGEOIS — A SEMI-HARD CHEESE WITH A LOVELY NUTTY FLAVOUR. TRADITIONALLY, IT IS MELTED WITH WHITE WINE AND GRAPPA OR KIRSCH AND SERVED WITH CHUNKS OF BREAD TO DIP INTO IT ALONGSIDE CHARCUTERIE AND PICKLES. THIS IS A MORE SUBTLE VERSION WITH BEER AND WHISKY, MAKING IT EVEN MORE DELICIOUS, IF THAT IS POSSIBLE. YOU REALLY DO NEED A FONDUE POT FOR THE BEST RESULTS, AS THE POT SITS ABOVE A FLAME THAT KEEPS THE CHEESE MELTED AND GENTLY BUBBLING. THEY ARE REALLY EASY TO PICK UP QUITE CHEAPLY SECOND-HAND.

Rub the garlic all over the inside of a fondue pot. Mix the cornflour/cornstarch with a little of the beer to make a smooth paste, then add this and the rest of the beer to the pot.

Put over a low heat, add the cheese and stir until it is melted and steaming but not boiling. If it is too thick you can add a little more beer. Add the whisky and then transfer to the fondue stand and light the burner.

Dip the slightly stale bread into the melting cheese and eat with lots of pickles and charcuterie.

CHEDDAR & CIDER FONDUE

ALTHOUGH THE CLASSIC FONDUE RECIPE IS SWISS, IT'S POSSIBLE TO MAKE IT WITH OTHER CHEESES.

270 g/3 cups grated Cheddar and 120 g/4 oz. soft
    ripened farmstead cheese, such as Brie, Camembert,
    or California Teleme, rind removed
2 teaspoons cornflour/cornstarch or potato flour
200 ml/¾ cup dry but fruity hard cider
1 tablespoon apple brandy or Calvados
freshly ground white or black pepper
crusty whole-wheat or granary rolls, cubed, to serve
apple wedges, to serve

Serves 2–3

Toss the cheese with the cornflour/cornstarch. Set aside until it has come to room temperature.

Start off the fondue on the hob/stovetop. Pour the cider into a fondue pan and heat until almost boiling. Remove from the heat and tip in about one-third of the cheese. Keep breaking up the cheese with a wooden spoon using a figure of eight motion. (Stirring it round and round as you do with a sauce makes it more likely that the cheese will separate).

Once the cheese has begun to melt, return it to a very low heat, stirring continuously. Gradually add the remaining cheese until you have a smooth, thick mass (this takes about 10 minutes, less with practice). If it seems too thick, add some more hot cider. Add the brandy and season with white pepper. Place over a fondue burner and serve with the cubes of bread. Use long fondue forks to dip the bread in, stirring the fondue often to prevent it solidifying.

BAKED HONEY & THYME CAMEMBERT WITH CRUDITÉS

HOW TO MAKE FRIENDS AND INFLUENCE PEOPLE? SERVE THEM THIS OOZING, MELTED CHEESE WITH A SELECTION OF COLOURFUL CHOPPED VEGETABLES, APPLE SLICES AND SOURDOUGH BREAD.

1 x 250-g/9-oz. Camembert
leaves from 2 sprigs of fresh thyme
2 tablespoons runny honey
1 red (bell) pepper, sliced into 1-cm/½-in. pieces
1 Granny Smith apple, cored and sliced into 8 wedges
1 large carrot, cut into 3-cm/1¼-in. fingers
sourdough bread, to serve

Serves 2–4

Preheat the oven to 200°C (400°F) Gas 6.

Score the top of the Camembert with a sharp knife, but leave the cheese in the box.

Push the thyme leaves into the scores, then drizzle over the honey.

Replace the lid, loosely, and place the box on a sheet pan.

Bake the Camembert in the preheated oven for 20 minutes until the cheese is all melted and wobbles when you move the sheet pan gently.

Serve the Camembert with the (bell) pepper, apple and carrot crudités and sourdough bread.

CHEDDAR & CALVADOS FONDUE WITH APPLE RÖSTI

185 ml/¾ cup dry cider
400 g/scant 4½ cups grated/
   shredded Cheddar
1 tablespoon plain/all-purpose flour
2–4 tablespoons Calvados
freshly ground black pepper
crispy fried bacon, to serve
   (optional)

FOR THE APPLE RÖSTI
3–4 potatoes,
   about 500 g/1 lb. 2 oz.
2 apples, about 300 g/
   10 oz., peeled
freshly squeezed juice of 1 lemon
½ teaspoon sea salt
freshly ground black pepper
1 tablespoon olive oil

Serves 6

POTATO RÖSTI (PANCAKES) ARE A VERY TRADITIONAL SWISS DISH, AS IS FONDUE. THIS APPLE VERSION OF A RÖSTI IS THE PERFECT FLAVOUR MATCH FOR A RICH CHEDDAR FONDUE, FLAVOURED WITH THE FIERY APPLE BRANDY, CALVADOS. SERVE WITH CRISPY FRIED BACON FOR EXTRA INDULGENCE, IF YOU LIKE.

To make the rösti, grate the potatoes on the coarse side of a box grater, put into a bowl, cover with water and let soak for 10 minutes. Drain in a colander, then transfer to a clean kitchen cloth and squeeze out very well. Grate the apples into the bowl, add the lemon juice to stop discolouration, toss well, then squeeze out in a clean kitchen cloth. Put the potato and apple back into a clean dry bowl, add the salt and pepper and mix well.

Put half the oil into a frying pan/skillet, heat well, add the potato mixture, press down with a fork and reduce the heat to medium-low. Cook for 10 minutes until brown, loosen with a palette knife/metal spatula, then turn out onto a large plate. Wipe around the pan, add the remaining oil and slide the rösti back into the pan. Cook for a further 10 minutes until cooked through. Keep warm in the oven until needed.

Pour the cider into a fondue pot and bring to the boil. Reduce the heat to simmering. Put the grated/shredded cheese and flour into a bowl and toss with a fork. Gradually add the cheese to the pot, stirring constantly, letting each addition melt into the cider. When creamy and smooth, add the Calvados and pepper to taste.

To serve, slice the rösti into 12, put 2 wedges onto each warmed plate, and top with bacon, if using, and a ladle of the hot fondue.

BLUE CHEESE FONDUE WITH WALNUT GRISSINI

125 ml/½ cup sweet white wine such as German Riesling or Gewürztraminer

400 g/14 oz. creamy blue cheese, such as Gorgonzola or Roquefort, coarsely chopped

1 teaspoon cornflour/cornstarch mixed with 1 tablespoon of the wine

FOR THE WALNUT GRISSINI

375 g/generous 2¾ cups unbleached plain/all-purpose flour, plus extra for rolling

1 sachet (7 g/¼ oz.) fast-action dried yeast

70 g/½ cup fresh walnuts

1 teaspoon sea salt

2 tablespoons walnut oil

TO SERVE

4–6 ripe pears, quartered, or 24 asparagus spears, lightly cooked

Serves 6

BLUE CHEESE, FRESH WALNUTS AND JUICY PEARS MAKE A DELICIOUS COMBINATION. THIS FONDUE IS PERFECT SERVED AS AN APPETIZER WITH ASPARAGUS, OR AS A DESSERT WITH PEARS.

To make the walnut grissini, put the flour, yeast, walnuts and salt into a food processor fitted with a plastic blade. With the machine running, add the oil and 200 ml/¾ cup water through the feed tube. Process in 15-second bursts until it forms a soft mass. Turn out onto a floured board and knead for 2 minutes. Put the dough into an oiled bowl, cover and let rest for 1 hour.

Preheat the oven to 200°C (400°F) Gas 6.

Knead again lightly, flatten to a rectangle about 40 x 15 cm/16 x 6 inches, then cut crossways into 1-cm/⅜-inch strips. Roll and stretch out each strip to about 30 cm/12 inches and transfer to a baking sheet (you will need to bake in two batches). Cook in the preheated oven for 16–18 minutes. Let cool on a wire rack. Serve immediately or store in an airtight container for 1 week.

To prepare the fondue, pour the wine into a small metal fondue pot and heat until simmering. Gradually stir in the blue cheese, then the cornflour/cornstarch mixture, stirring constantly until smooth. Transfer the pot to its tabletop burner and serve with walnut grissini and pears or asparagus.

PUMPKIN FONDUE

1 large red or orange pumpkin, about 30 cm/12 inches in diameter, or 4 small, round Red Onion squash or similar
3–4 tablespoons olive oil
a few torn fresh thyme sprigs or sage leaves
salt and freshly ground black pepper

FOR THE FONDUE

2 teaspoons potato flour or cornflour/cornstarch
300 ml/1¼ cups dry white wine, such as Riesling or Grüner Veltliner, or dry cider
1 garlic clove, peeled and halved
1 bay leaf
400 g/14 oz. Gruyère (or similar), derinded and thinly sliced or grated/shredded
2 tablespoons Kirsch (optional)
250–300 g/9–10 oz. Taleggio or Fontina cheese, derinded and thinly sliced or grated/shredded
4 tablespoons double/heavy cream or crème fraîche

Serves 4

SERVING FONDUE IN A BAKED PUMPKIN SHELL IS NOT JUST ABOUT FUN PRESENTATION – THE SWEET, TENDER SQUASH IS WONDERFUL WITH THE SALTY, SHARP RICHNESS OF THE CHEESE. EITHER USE A WHOLE, LARGE PUMPKIN FOR EVERYONE TO DIP INTO OR SMALL INDIVIDUAL SQUASHES. SERVE WITH CUBES OF CRUSTY BREAD FOR DIPPING AND SPOONS FOR SCRAPING THE BAKED SQUASH FROM THE SHELL. THE CHEESE YOU USE IS UP TO YOU, BUT A MIXTURE OF A GRUYÈRE-LIKE CHEESE WITH A SOFTER CHEESE SUCH AS TALEGGIO OR FONTINA WORKS WELL.

Preheat the oven to 190°C (375°F) Gas 5.

Cut a lid off the pumpkin or the squashes and, if necessary, take a thin slice off the base so that the shell(s) will stand upright.

Scoop out the seeds and enough flesh to leave a shell about 2.5 cm/ 1 inch thick (Red Onion squash are fine as they are, just remove the seeds). Rub with the oil inside and out, season with salt and pepper, add a few herb sprigs to the cavity and bake in the preheated oven for about 50 minutes for a large pumpkin or 40 minutes for small squash. Bake the lids as well, if liked, for around 20–25 minutes, depending on size.

Meanwhile, make the cheese fondue. Mix the potato flour or cornstarch/cornflour with 2–3 tablespoons of the wine and set aside. Put the remaining wine in a medium-sized, heavy-based saucepan over medium heat and bring to the boil. Simmer for 2–3 minutes, then add the garlic and bay leaf and reduce the heat. Add the Gruyère and, stirring all the time, allow it to melt. When melted, remove and discard the garlic and bay leaf then stir in the potato flour mixture and the Kirsch (if using) until smooth. Add the Taleggio and stir frequently over low heat until the cheese melts. Add the cream, season to taste and stir over the heat until you have a smooth, velvety texture.

To serve, pour the fondue into the baked shell(s), cover with the lid(s), if using, and carry to the table.

FONDUTA

THE ITALIAN VERSION OF FONDUE IS A SPECIALITY OF THE VALLE D'AOSTA IN THE NORTH-WEST. IT IS MADE WITH FONTINA CHEESE, ENRICHED WITH EGG YOLKS, THEN SCATTERED DECADENTLY WITH SHAVINGS OF WHITE TRUFFLES FROM NEIGHBOURING PIEDMONT. IF YOU DON'T HAVE A TRUFFLE TO HAND, A SPRINKLING OF TRUFFLE OIL WILL GIVE A HINT OF THE PRIZED FRAGRANCE.

½ teaspoon cornflour/cornstarch
250 ml/1 cup milk
500 g/1 lb. 2 oz. grated/
    shredded Fontina
50 g/3½ tablespoons unsalted
    butter (optional)
4 egg yolks
freshly ground white pepper
1 white truffle (optional)
    or truffle oil

TO SERVE
steamed spring vegetables such
    as baby carrots, baby leeks,
    baby turnips, asparagus,
    fennel and mangetout/
    snow peas, cut into bite-sized
    pieces if necessary
toast or polenta triangles

Serves 6

Put the cornflour/cornstarch into a small bowl, add 1 tablespoon of the milk and stir until dissolved – this is called 'slaking'.

Put the remaining milk into the top section of a double boiler, then add the cheese and slaked cornflour/cornstarch. Put over a saucepan of simmering water and heat, stirring constantly, until the cheese melts. Stir in the butter, if using, and remove from the heat.

Put the egg yolks into a bowl and whisk lightly. Whisk in a few tablespoons of the hot cheese mixture to warm the yolks. Pour this mixture back into the double boiler, stirring vigorously. Return the saucepan to the heat and continue stirring until the mixture thickens.

To serve, ladle the cheese mixture into preheated bowls and sprinkle with freshly ground white pepper and shavings of truffle, if using. Alternatively, sprinkle with a few drops of truffle oil. Serve the bowls surrounded by the prepared vegetables, with toast or polenta triangles for dipping.

RACLETTE

1.2 kg/2 lb. 11 oz. waxy
    new potatoes
1-kg/2 lb. 4-oz. piece of raclette
gherkins, pickled silverskin
    onions, cured meats and
    salamis, to serve
salt and freshly ground
    black pepper

FOR THE TOMATO SALAD
6 large vine tomatoes, sliced
1 garlic clove, crushed
1 tablespoon red wine vinegar
good pinch of sugar
4 tablespoons extra-virgin
    olive oil
2 tablespoons freshly chopped
    parsley leaves

FOR THE GREEN SALAD
2 tablespoons white wine
    or cider vinegar
1 teaspoon Dijon mustard
4 tablespoons extra-virgin
    olive oil
2 tablespoons crème fraîche
1 large head of soft green lettuce

raclette grill

Serves 6

THE WORD RACLETTE IS THE NAME OF AN INCREDIBLE SWISS CHEESE AND THE DISH YOU USE IT FOR. RACLETTE CHEESE IS A WASHED-RIND, EXTREMELY MELTY CHEESE THAT COMES IN LARGE WHEELS. ALL OVER SWITZERLAND, VILLAGES HAVE THEIR OWN STYLE OF RACLETTE CHEESE, AND EACH VILLAGE HOTLY CONTESTS THAT THEIRS IS THE BEST. A LAYER FROM A WEDGE OF THE CHEESE IS MELTED AGAINST A HEATED ELEMENT AND SCRAPED OFF USING A SPATULA (THE WORD *RACLEUR* MEANING TO 'SCRAPE') ONTO AWAITING JUST-BOILED POTATOES. IT IS SERVED WITH AIR-DRIED HAMS AND SALAMIS, CORNICHONS AND PICKLED SILVERSKIN ONIONS. MAKE SURE YOU EAT THE RINDY BITS AND DON'T PUSH THEM TO ONE SIDE, AS THEY ARE PACKED WITH THE BEST FLAVOUR.

Cook the potatoes in boiling salted water until tender. Drain well. Line a bowl with a clean kitchen towel, tip the potatoes into it and wrap them up to keep warm.

Meanwhile, make the salads. For the tomato salad, put the tomatoes on a platter. Whisk the garlic, red wine vinegar, sugar and seasoning in a small bowl then gradually add the oil. Pour over the tomatoes and scatter with the parsley.

For the green salad, whisk the vinegar and mustard together with plenty of seasoning. Whisk in the oil and crème fraîche. Loosen with a little water if you need to. Wash the lettuce and put in a serving bowl. Pour over the dressing and toss.

Melt the exposed side of the raclette cheese against the grill of a raclette machine. Once melting and bubbling, put a few potatoes on a plate and scrape a layer of the cheesy goodness on top of the potatoes. Repeat for the next plate.

Eat with the salads, cured meats and pickles.

CAULIFLOWER & GRUYÈRE SOUP

TRY AND FIND A SMALL, WHOLE HEAD OF CAULIFLOWER THAT IS CREAMY-WHITE AND SOFT FOR THIS GORGEOUSLY CHEESY SOUP.

30 g/2 tablespoons butter
1 onion, roughly chopped
1 celery stalk, chopped
1 small cauliflower, about 1 kg/2 lb. 4 oz., cut into small pieces
1.5 litres/6 cups vegetable or chicken stock
250 ml/1 cup double/ heavy cream

200 g/scant 2 cups grated/ shredded Gruyère, plus extra to serve
salt and freshly ground black pepper
freshly chopped parsley and toasted wholemeal bread, to serve

Serves 4

Heat the butter in a saucepan over high heat. Add the onion and celery, and cook for about 5 minutes, until the onion has softened but not browned.

Add the cauliflower pieces and stock, and bring to the boil. Allow to boil for 25–30 minutes, until the cauliflower is really soft and breaking up in the stock.

Transfer the mixture to a food processor or blender and process the mixture in batches until smooth. Return the purée to a clean saucepan. Add the cream and cheese, and cook over low heat, stirring constantly, until the cheese has all smoothly melted into the soup.

Season to taste with a little sea salt and black pepper. Serve sprinkled with chopped parsley and extra cheese, and with buttered wholemeal toast on the side.

BROCCOLI & BLUE CHEESE SOUP

MRS BELLS BLUE IS A SOFT BLUE BRITISH CHEESE BY SHEPHERDS PURSE CHEESES. YOU CAN USE ANY MID-STRENGTH BLUE CHEESE AS AN ALTERNATIVE.

50 g/3½ tablespoons butter
6 banana shallots, finely chopped
3 potatoes, peeled and diced
4 celery sticks, sliced
1.5 litres/6 cups chicken stock
950 g/2 lbs. 2 oz. purple sprouting or new-season tender broccoli

400 g/14 oz. Mrs Bells Blue or other creamy blue cheese, such as Stilton
pinch of grated nutmeg
200 ml/¾ cup double/ heavy cream
ground black pepper
croutons, to serve

Serves 6

Melt the butter in a large saucepan, add the shallots and cook gently for a few minutes to soften. Add the potatoes and celery, and stir to coat well with the butter. Add the stock and bring the liquid to the boil, then simmer for 15–20 minutes, until the potato is almost tender.

Add the broccoli and continue to cook for a further 3–5 minutes, until the stalks are tender. It is crucial not to overcook the broccoli or you lose the lovely bright green colour. Purée the soup immediately with a blender. When smooth, crumble in three-quarters of the blue cheese and add a pinch of nutmeg and a good twist of black pepper, to season. Stir in almost all of the cream, reserving a little to garnish.

Ladle the soup into bowls, garnish with a swirl of cream and crumble over the remaining blue cheese. Serve immediately, with croutons.

FRENCH ONION SOUP WITH COMTÉ TOASTS

MOLTEN COMTÉ, WITH ITS NUTTY, EARTHY TASTE AND CREAMY TEXTURE, IS THE IDEAL CHOICE FOR THESE OOZING TOASTS THAT SOAK UP THE RICH BROTH OF THE ONION SOUP TO PERFECTION.

25 g/2 tablespoons unsalted butter
3 tablespoons olive oil
1 kg/2 lb. 4 oz. large onions, very thinly sliced
250 ml/generous 1 cup dry white wine
1 litre/quart rich beef stock
good pinch of grated nutmeg
small handful of fresh thyme sprigs
2 fresh bay leaves
75 ml/⅓ cup good-quality Madeira
1 day-old baguette or other crusty bread, cut into slices
1 garlic clove, peeled
150 g/5 oz. Comté cheese, grated/shredded
salt and freshly ground black pepper

Serves 4

Melt the butter in a heavy-based pan or flameproof casserole dish and add the oil. Add the onions and season with salt. Cook over low heat, stirring occasionally, for at least 45 minutes until they have reduced right down to a golden, sticky mass.

Add the wine and bubble, stirring, for a minute, then add the beef stock, a good grating of nutmeg and the herbs. Simmer for about 20 minutes, then add the Madeira and bubble for 5 minutes more. Check the seasoning and spoon into four small ovenproof bowls or dishes.

Preheat the grill/broiler to high.

Toast the slices of crusty bread and rub one side all over with the garlic. Put the toasts on top of the bowls so that they cover the surface of the soup. Sprinkle with lots and lots of cheese and put on a baking sheet under the grill/broiler until the soup is bubbling and the cheese toasts are melted and golden. Serve straight away.

SPINACH & PARMESAN SOUP WITH NUTMEG & ROSEMARY

THIS RECIPE USES THE ROBUST FLAVOUR OF PARMESAN, BUT ANY OTHER HARD, STRONG CHEESE WOULD DO INSTEAD. YOU CAN USE THE TENDER, WASHED BAGS OF SPINACH WE FIND IN OUR GROCERY STORES OR A TOUGHER VARIETY SUCH AS EPINARD, WITH THE TOUGH STALKS TRIMMED AWAY.

50 g/3½ tablespoons butter
6 strong shallots, chopped
2 garlic cloves, crushed
1 large potato, peeled and diced
2 tablespoons chopped fresh
   rosemary leaves, plus extra
   sprigs to garnish
1.5 litres/6 cups chicken stock
1 kg/2 lbs. 4 oz. spinach leaves,
   any really coarse stalks
   removed and chopped
   to a manageable size
pinch of grated nutmeg,
   plus extra to garnish
200 g/2⅔ cups freshly grated
   Parmesan, or other hard
   strong cheese
few tablespoons of crème fraîche,
   to taste
salt and freshly ground
   black pepper

Serves 6-8

In a large saucepan, melt the butter and gently cook the shallots with the garlic for a few minutes, until softened. Add the potato and rosemary, cover with the stock and bring to a simmer. Cook for 15–20 minutes, until the potato is tender. Add the spinach to the pan and bring to the boil, then draw the pan off the heat and blend everything well with a stick blender. Add a grating of nutmeg, to taste, and season well with salt and pepper. Stir in the Parmesan and most of the crème fraîche, to enrich the soup.

Ladle the soup into bowls and serve garnished with a dusting of nutmeg, a spoonful of the remaining crème fraîche and sprigs of fresh rosemary.

INDEX

CREDITS